The Wayfaring Stranger's Notebook

The Wayfaring Stranger's Notebook

BURL IVES

THE **BOBBS-MERRILL** COMPANY, INC.
A SUBSIDIARY OF **HOWARD W. SAMS & CO., INC.**
Publishers · INDIANAPOLIS · NEW YORK

Library of Congress Catalog Card Number: 62-10017
Copyright © 1962 by Burl Ives
All Rights Reserved
Manufactured in the United States of America
First Printing, 1962

CONTENTS

The Wayfaring Stranger's Notebook

PREFATORY TO WHAT FOLLOWS

When I was a college student I could not become interested in historical facts. It was only when I had occasion to read the writings of early Americans themselves—say from the time the first settlement was made to the middle of the nineteenth century—and found inscriptions, descriptions, and analyses contemporary to their times that I acquired a much more intent and immediate feeling for the life of historical times than any history book, no matter how vivid its narrative, had been able to give me. It was during my search through the music of our country's past that I was led quite accidentally to the writings that opened to me the rich panorama of stories, pictures, and unique personalities that went into the making of America.

Although I am not primarily a teacher, a researcher, or a writer, but only a collector and singer of songs, I found myself collecting stories and tidbits of information as I went along from here and there and writing them down for my own amusement. I've put these down through the years more or less at random, without any idea of publication. Every once in a while I would show my growing notebook to friends and I always found them amused and interested by my recorded browsing. A friend of mine from Bobbs-Merrill happened on these one night when we were talking and thought that perhaps they would interest you, the public. I hope that this will be so.

I want to confess that as I sat and read I was almost never

11

alone. In my imagination, my dear uncle, Doctor Sam Icle Ivanhoe, was by my side, jogging my mind with his native American observations. Dr. Sam was a Johnsonian character out of my childhood, who made his living traveling back and forth across the country selling everything from corsets to patent medicines, from trinkets to trips to Europe. He had a comment and an attitude about everything, and often as I read, even to this day, pertinent statements of his come to mind.

Dr. Sam's observations, based upon his sense of America as a great country with a destiny, were derived from his identification with his maternal uncle, a figure famous in the United States and abroad since 1790. This was none other than Samson Icle, derisively cartooned as sticklike Uncle Sam of the high hat, protruding wrists, and striped trousers. Needless to say, *my* uncle, Dr. Sam, was as affluent and well-fed and well-clothed as *his* Uncle Sam was awkward and ill-appareled.

The caricatures of his Uncle Sam infuriated Dr. Sam, and he blamed it on early British jealousy. He never would join the "Anglo-American League" or the "Sons of the American Revolution" and would scowl at any member of these organizations saying, "I'm a Yankee just like you and I ain't ashamed owning to it. But you keep hankerin' back to your ancestors like you was ashamed of your broughtens up and I must say you are no great credit to them."

Dr. Sam would come to visit us when I was a child, and this event was always an occasion. It was not only his gaiety and irreverence, unusual to our little midwestern town, it was that the world was his to prowl, and humanity his interest. Sitting back with his eyes closed, he would make me recite the following which he painstakingly taught me when I was five years old:

> Since all men's deeds are infinite,
> It is sufficient to recite:
> Some end their parts when some begin;
> Some go out,—and some come in.
> Some are serving,—some commanding;

Some are sitting,—some are standing;
Some rejoicing,—some are grieving;
Some entreating,—some relieving;
Some are weeping,—some are laughing;
Some are thirsting,—some are quaffing;
Some accepting,—some refusing;
Some are thrifty,—some abusing;
Some compelling,—some persuading;
Some are flattering,—some degrading;
Some are patient,—some are fuming;
Some are modest,—some presuming;
Some are leasing,—some are farming;
Some are helping,—some are harming;
Some are running,—some are riding;
Some departing,—some abiding;
Some are sending,—some are bringing;
Some are crying,—some are singing;
Some are hearing,—some are preaching;
Some are learning,—some are teaching;
Some disdaining,—some affecting;
Some assiduous,—some neglecting;
Some are feasting,—some are fasting;
Some are saving,—some are wasting;
Some are losing,—some are winning;
Some repenting,—some are sinning;
Some professing,—some adoring;
Some are silent,—some are roaring;
Some are restive,—some are willing;
Some preserving,—some are killing;
Some are bounteous,—some are grinding;
Some are seeking,—some are finding;
Some are thieving,—some receiving;
Some are hiding,—some revealing;
Some commending,—some are blaming;
Some dismembering,—some new-framing;
Some are quiet,—some disputing;

Some confuted and confuting;
Some are marching,—some retiring;
Some are resting,—some aspiring;
Some enduring,—some deriding;
Some are falling,—some are rising.

I would stand in front of Dr. Sam waiting for the rare banana or orange that was my reward. Opening his blue eyes, looking full on me, he would give me my prize.

Dr. Sam explained words and things to me. He was a walking dictionary, yet he had such strength of conviction that what I herein pass on to you might best be termed my "Samsonary."

"I shall take you by the scruff of your curiosity," Dr. Sam often assured me on plumbing the depths of my ignorance, "that I might painlessly extract from your mind the quantum of light therein that has been given unto you to shed upon the tantum of marvels that Nature has placed around you."

And so it is, that what you will read, is not of my reflections alone.

CAPE COD: QUESTION MARK
OF A NATION-TO-BE

Walking leisurely along the dunes of Cape Cod, gazing in wonder at the surging Atlantic, I project myself in imagination to the deck of a little sailing vessel. I become an early explorer to whom sight of this little hook of land is my first view of a great continent. Parts of this curve of sand that formed an everlasting question mark to the future of the nation-to-be have remained unchanged.

Through the diary of a man named Gabriel Archer we can share in the discovery and naming of Cape Cod in May, 1602. His book, which appeared in London in 1605, was *The Relation of Captain Gosnold's Voyage; delivered by Gabriel Archer, a gentleman in said voyage.*

The fifteenth day of May we had again sight of the land, which made ahead, being as we thought an island, by reason of a large sound that appeared westward between it and the main, for coming to the west end thereof, we did perceive a large opening, we called it Shoal Hope. Near this cape we came to anchor in fifteen fathoms, where we took great store of codfish, for which we altered the name, and called it Cape Cod. Here we saw sculls of herring, mackerel, and other small fish, in great abundance. This is a low sandy shoal, but without danger, also we came to anchor again in sixteen fathoms, fair by the land in the latitude of 42 degrees. This cape is well near a mile broad, and lieth northeast by east. The captain went ashore here and found the ground to be full of pease, strawberries, whortle-berries, &c., as then unripe, the sand also by the shore somewhat deep, the firewood there by us taken in was of cypress, birch, witch-hazel and beech. A young Indian came here to the captain, armed with his bow and arrows, and had certain plates of copper hanging in his ears; he showed a willingness to help us in our occasions.

FATHER MARQUETTE'S MAGIC

I remember Dr. Sam was heating a poultice of dung for a horse infected with fly in the hoof, when I came to him and he related the story of Father Marquette. "Make the best use of what's on hand," Dr. Sam said, applying the steaming poultice to the horse's hoof. "A little nature and a touch of magic are sometimes the keys to man's estate."

Father Marquette, the Catholic priest, came to America with a Jesuit mission. He and Monsieur Joliet explored the Mississippi River in 1637, wrote a long, instructive narrative of their trip and prepared the maps that became the wedge that opened the river to others.

On one trip, Father Marquette and a companion, Sieur Du Lhut, were captured by the Ojibways. The story, as Dr. Sam put it together, is this:

Father Marquette insisted on going into the Ojibway village, although he had been warned they were hostile. He and his companion entered and received no greeting. They were surrounded by silent hostility. White Otter, the chief, did not rise to greet them but remained seated on his throne of deer and bear skins.

"Why have you come to the land of the Ojibway?" he demanded. "Speak the truth."

Father Marquette, who spoke the language, explained his peaceful mission was to bring God's word.

White Otter rose and commanded his warriors, "Seize the black coat and his men. Bind them. They die tomorrow."

Father Marquette and his companion were bound and gagged. Unable to move or speak, they were taken to a bare wigwam and thrown on the ground. There was no way for them to loosen their bindings or communicate with each other. They slept out of sheer exhaustion in spite of the pain and discomfort.

In the night, White Otter's daughter, Wanena, who probably had never heard of Pocahontas, cut their bonds commanding, "Follow. Be silent. Be slow. Make no noise. Break no twig. Move silent as the wildcat or we die."

She led the men from the camp through the forest. "I have a canoe to take us to the Holy Isle," she said. "There we will make offerings before the Great Manitou and ask his help. There friendly red men will come and rescue us. Many nations come to the Holy Isle."

At the Holy Isle they pulled the canoe up into the reeds to hide it from searching eyes. Wanena led them through the forest into a clearing. In the dim light of dawn stood the rudely carved figure of the great god Manitou. The figure was made of pine, rising six feet high, its body covered with bright feathers woven from dry reeds. Around the feet of the idol were weapons, bows, and food offerings.

The sun rose and shone brightly upon the feather dress, and the feathers glistened with many colors.

Wanena clutched the arm of Du Lhut. "Listen," she whispered, "I hear steps." The two men listened but heard nothing. "Quickly! Fly!" she begged, and started to run. When they did not follow her, she stopped at the edge of the forest. Then before they could make a move, White Otter and eight of his warriors were upon them. Du Lhut seized one of the spears lying before the idol and, prepared to sell his life dearly, stood with his back to the figure. Father Marquette drew forth his crucifix and prayed. On the edge of the forest, Wanena dropped to the ground, drew her blanket over her head and began to sing the death song of the Ojibways.

White Otter was furious. "The black coat and the woman must die before the Great Manitou!"

Wanena keened her song, expecting at any second to receive the blow which would send her to the Great Spirit. Du Lhut stood ready to do battle.

Father Marquette answered for them all. "We will defy you and your god. I do not fear death if my God wills it." The priest went on, "I could deliver us as easily as I could destroy that worthless image you call the Great Manitou." Father Marquette turned and spoke in Latin to Du Lhut, who dropped his spear and slowly walked to the priest's side. The father turned again to the Indians. "I challenge your god to withstand mine," he said.

White Otter was contemptuous. "You have said this before to the Indians. You would play a game before you die? Very good! Let your god destroy the Great Manitou."

Father Marquette flourished his cross twice in the air. "I pray to my God to send fire from the sky and burn this image." He turned to White Otter. "If my God does so, will you set us free? Will you become a Christian?"

"If your god burns the Great Manitou, yes. If you fail, you die."

"And you will pardon your daughter?" Father Marquette pointed to the girl who was still chanting the death song.

By this time the sun was high in the sky and burning fiercely, for it was midsummer. There were sweet odors from the wood, and insects hummed as they flew to and fro among the wild flowers. Father Marquette raised his crucifix above his head. Beside him, Du Lhut did the same. They stood for a while, hands raised above their heads; then Father Marquette said in a loud voice, using White Otter's own tongue, "In the name of God, I command fire to destroy this idol."

Soon a small spot of light danced on the breast of the idol, then moved to its stomach. The light grew bright and steady.

Soon smoke began to gather around the light. Father Marquette called more loudly, more dramatically, and the smoke grew heavier. A flame suddenly burst out from the light and soon the feathers and reeds were on fire. A breeze came up quickly fanning through the feathers.

"Spare us, O mighty medicine man," cried the Indians.

"The white men's God is greater than the Great Manitou!" cried White Otter who was on his knees in terror as were his braves.

As the image of the Great Manitou burned to the ground, the red men laid down their weapons and were baptized in a nearby brook by the priest, and for many days he stayed with them, teaching them and explaining the laws by which they were to live.

Father Marquette's missionary work among the Indians of this area was much easier after this event became known, and he received full cooperation from White Otter. He had used faith and his wits. His most treasured possession, his crystal crucifix, was a good magnifying glass.

HENRY HUDSON'S MEN

"You might as well try to whittle John L. Sullivan down a foot by calling him a 'donkey,'" Dr. Sam said, "as expect to obtain a peace pipe from an Indian by calling him a 'savage.'"

Robert Juet, one of the crew accompanying Captain Hudson, kept a diary, excerpts from which show clearly the lack of understanding with which the explorers looked at the Indians:

1609, Sept. 6. Our master sent John Colman with four men to sound the river, four leagues distant, which they did, but in their return to the ship, they were set upon by Indians in two canoes, to the number of 26; in which affair John Colman was killed by an arrow shot into his throat, and two others were wounded. The next day Colman was buried on a point of land which to this day bears his name.

Sept. 8. The people came on board us, and brought tobacco and Indian wheat, to exchange for knives and beads, and offered us no violence. So we, fitting up our boat, did mark them, to see if they would make any show of the death of our man, but they did not.

Sept. 9. In the morning two great canoes came on board full of men; one with bows and arrows, and the other in show of buying knives to betray us; but we perceived their intention. We took two of them, to have kept them, and put red coats on them, and would not suffer the others to come near us, and soon after the canoes leave them. Immediately two other natives came on board us; one we took, and let the other go, but he soon escaped by jumping overboard.

Sept. 11. The people of the country came on board, making show of love, and gave us tobacco and Indian wheat.

Sept. 12. This morning there came eight-and-twenty canoes full of men, women and children to betray us; but we saw their intent, and suffered none of them to come on board. They have great tobacco pipes of yellow copper, and pots of earth to dress their meat in.

Sept. 15. This morning the two captive savages got out of a port of the ship and made their escape.

Sept. 18. The master's mate went on shore with an old Indian, a sachem of the country, who took him to his house and treated him kindly.

Oct. 1. One man in a canoe kept hanging under the stern of the ship, and would not be driven off. He soon contrived to climb up by the rudder, and got into the cabin window, which had been left open, from which he stole a pillow, two shirts, and two bandoleers. The mate shot him in the breast and killed him. Many others were in canoes about the ship, who immediately fled, and some jumped overboard. A boat manned from the ship pursued them, and coming up with one in the water, he laid hold of the side of the boat, and endeavored to overset it; at which one in the boat cutt off his hands with a sword, and he was drowned.

Oct. 2. Came one of the savages that swam away from us at our going up the river, with many others, thinking to betray us, but we suffered none of them to enter our ship. Whereupon two canoes, full of men with their bows and arrows, shot at us after our stern; in recompense whereof we discharged six muskets and killed two or three of them. Then above an hundred of them came to a point of land to shoot at us. There I shot a falcon at them, killed two of them; whereupon the rest fled into the woods. Yet they manned off another canoe with nine or ten men, which came to meet us; so I shot at it also a falcon, and shot it through, and killed one of them. Then our men, with their muskets, killed three or four more of them.

TOBACCO'S BUT AN INDIAN WEED

The Indian plant, tobacco, was introduced into England about 1565. Discussion of the new habit of smoking was heated, in pamphlets and song. The smoke was swallowed, hence, the reference in the song to drinking tobacco.

A popular couplet from the reign of James I read: "Musicke, tobacco, sacke and Sleepe, The tide of sorrow backward keepe." And in King George's times, they described it "but an Indian weed" and sang:

> Tobacco's but an Indian weed,
> Grows green at morn, cut down at eve.
>> It shows our decay;
>> We are but clay;
> Think of this, when you drink tobacco.

> The pipe that is so lily-white,
> Wherein so many take delight,
>> Gone with a touch,
>> Man's life is such,
> Think on this, when you drink tobacco.

> The pipe that is so foul within,
> Shows how the soul is stained with sin;

It doth require
the purging fire.
Think on this, when you drink tobacco.

The ashes that are left behind,
Do serve to put us all in mind,
That unto dust,
Return we must,
Think on this, when you drink tobacco.

The smoke that doth so high ascend,
Shows that our life must have an end;
The vapour's gone,
Man's life is done.
Think on this, when you drink tobacco.

THE FIRST PILGRIM CHRISTMAS

"Christmas is a time of great wonder to me," Dr. Sam used to say, "of peace on earth and good will to men. And it's a great wonder that men don't take the time out in peace and good will while they are on earth, that the Man did, whom they remember at Christmas."

In my experience, the celebration of Christmas has many facets, religious wonder, humility, family fun. . . . We are so used to celebrating Christmas as a gay occasion and a holiday that it comes as a shock to realize that when the Pilgrims came to America, this was not their custom. A sober page from William Bradford's diary reports on the Pilgrim's first Christmas Day at Plymouth Colony:

> The day called Christmas Day ye Govr cal'd them out to worke (as was used) but ye moste of this new company excuse themselves, and saie yt went against their consciences to work on yt Day. So ye Govr tould them that if they made it mater of conscience, he would spare them till they were better informed. So he led away yt rest and left them; but when they came home at noon from their work he found them in ye street at play openly, some pitching ye bar, and some at stool-ball and such like sports. So he went to them and took away their implements and tould them it was against his conscience that they should play and others work.

A NON-PURITANICAL COLONY

Puritan and Pilgrim New England lived side by side for a time with an English colony that is rarely spoken of because, I suppose, our historians are ashamed of it. They are still too puritanical to give much attention to its existence. The name of this colony was first "Mary-Mount" and then "Merrymount." It was unsanctified in the eyes of the more religious colonists, for the people at Merrymount were Episcopals who had pancakes at Shrovetide! Wassail at Christmas! And they were known to have erected the Maypole!

The story of Merrymount is that in 1625, Captain Wollaston, a wealthy young Englishman, came to Quincy, Massachusetts, with a retinue for a plantation. He would have been better fitted to a life in the southern colonies although, even there, his tendency to gaiety might have been frowned upon.

However, he liked the New England scene and settled. His New England plantation might have continued to thrive had not he decided in a few years to make a visit to the colony of Virginia. He chartered a boat, and to pay for his trip, took along a group of his servants to sell to the Jamestown planters for the remaining period of their indenture.

Now among the indentured servants who stayed behind was a young lawyer named Thomas Morton who had come to Merrymount out of debtors' jail in London. No sooner had Wollaston left, than Morton took command of the colony by keeping Wollaston's lieutenant under lock and key.

It somehow came to nearby Boston's attention that Morton and his people were drinking and consorting with Indian women! This was not enough—it was finally brought to the public attention that he had erected a Maypole around which much "licentious action" was taking place. Endicott and a group of Puritans decided to investigate.

On an early May day in 1628, the Merrymount inhabitants were dancing about their Maypole. They had a circle, a Lord and Lady of the Revels, and a mock clergyman to join the pair in wedlock. Dancing around the Maypole, they sang:

> Drink and be merry, merry, merry boys,
> Let all your delight be in Hymen's joys,
> Io to Hymen now the day is come,
> About the merry Maypole take a room.
>
> Make green garlands, bring bottles out;
> And fill sweet Nectar freely about,
> Uncover thy head and fear no harm,
> For here's good liquor to keep it warm.
>
> Nectar is a thing assigned,
> By the Deities own mind
> To cure the heart oppressed with grief,
> And of good liquors is the chief.
>
> Give to the melancholy man,
> A cup or two of't now and then.
> This physic will soon revive his blood
> And Make him be of a merrier mood.
>
> Give to the nymph that's free from scorn,
> No Irish stuff, nor Scotch oler worn;
> Lasses in beaver coats come away,
> Ye shall be welcome to us night and day.

Suddenly the bells and the laughter were silenced, for one after the other they turned and saw a band of frowning Puritans watching their sport from a nearby wood. They were silent and fearful, for Puritan wrath was a dread thing.

In the silence, Endicott walked through them and hacked down the Maypole with his sword. "So shall fall the pride of vain people," he said, and then he ordered his companions to tie the men to the trees where they were given six dozen blows apiece.

The Maypole at Merrymount was not set up again although worldly music, plays, and dancing went on. All of this, however, would not have occasioned more than a scandal, but it was soon learned that Merrymount was cornering the fur trade. Morton had done this by selling firearms to the Indians, vowing that his purpose was to increase the amount of beavers that they brought him.

It truly did increase his accumulation of beavers. So much so that the Puritans brought to bear on him a law that declared the sale of firearms to Indians forbidden in all the colonies. Accordingly, Miles Standish was sent to capture Morton—which he did. This ended the little experiment in high living at Merrymount Colony which, since Morton left and Wollaston failed to return, soon became part of the forest again.

Thomas Morton, the leader of the revelers at Merrymount, tells his side of the story in his book, published at Amsterdam in 1637, *New English Canaan:*

> The inhabitants of Pasonagesset (having translated the name of their habitation from that ancient salvage name to Ma-reMount; and being resolved to have the new name confirmed for a memorial to after ages) did devise amongst themselves to have it performed in a solemne manner with Revels, & merriment after the old English custome; prepared to sett up a Maypole. . & therefore brewed a barrell of excellent beare, & provided a case of bottles to be spent,

with other good cheare, for all commers of that day. And because they would have it in a compleat forme, they had prepared a song fitting to the time and present occasion.

And upon Mayday they brought the Maypole to the place appointed, with drumes, gunnes, pistols, and other fitting instruments, for that purpose; and there erected it with the help of salvages, that came thether of purpose to see the manner of our Revels. A goodly pine tree of 80. foote long, was reared up, with a peare of buckshorns nayled one, somewhat near onto the top of it: where it stood as a faire sea marke for directions; how to finde out the way of mine Hoste of Ma-reMount.

. . . The setting up of this Maypole was a lamentable specticale to the precise seperatists: that lived at new Plimmouth. They termed it an Idoll; yea they called it the Calfe of Horeb: and stood at defiance with the place, naming it Mount Dagon; threatening to make it a woeful mount and not a merry mount . . .

There was likewise a merry song made, which (to make their Revells more fashionable) was sung with a Corus, every man bearing his part; which they performed in a daunce, hand in hand about the Maypole, whiles one of the Company sung, and filled out the good liquor like Gammedes and Jupiter.

William Bradford, the governor of the "precise seperatists at Plimmouth," tells a somewhat different version of the revels at Merrymount, with a much less tolerant view of "mine honest Hoste," Mr. Morton. According to William Bradford's *History of Plymouth Plantation*, Mr. Morton had a part of the plantation of Captain Wollaston, which was not working out very well.

Having continued there some time, and not finding things to answer their expectations, nor profit to arise as they looked for, Captain Wollaston takes a great part of the servants, and transports them to Virginia, where he puts them off at good rates, selling their time to other men.

30

In the absence of Captain Wollaston, this Mr. Morton, "having more craft than honesty" harangues the rest of the plantation.

"You see," saith he, "that many of you fellows are carried off to Virginia; and if you stay . . you will also be carried away and sold for slaves with the rest. . . . I, having a part in the plantation, will receive you as my partners and consociates; so may you be free from service, and we will converse, trade, plant, and live together as equals, and support and protect one another," or to like effect. This counsel was easily received.

. . . After this they fell to great licentiousness, and led a dissolute life, pouring out themselves into all profaneness. And Morton became lord of misrule, and maintained (as it were) a school of Atheism. And after they had got some goods into their hands, and got much by trade with the Indians, they spent it as vainly, in quaffing and drinking both wine and strong waters in great excess, and, as some reported, ten shillings worth in a morning. They also set up a May-pole, drinking and dancing about it many days together, inviting the Indian women, for their consorts, dancing and frisking together (like so many fairies, or furies rather), and worse practices . . .

. . . They changed also the name of their place, and instead of calling it Mount Wollaston, they called it Merry Mount, as if this jollity would have lasted ever. But this continued not long, for . . . shortly after came over that worthy gentleman, Mr. John Endicott . . . who visiting those parts caused that May-pole to be cut down and rebuked them for their profaneness, and admonished them to look there should be better walking; so they now, or others, changed the name of their place again, and called it Mount Dagon.

"To maintain this riotous prodigality and profuse excess," Morton took to trading "pieces, powder, and shot to the Indians," much to the apprehension of the other plantations. The Indians became very adept at hunting with guns, "so as they became far more active in that employment than any of the English, by reason of their swiftness of foot, and nimbleness of body, being also quick sighted, and by continual exercise well knowing the haunts of all sorts of game."

As for the Indians:

When they saw the execution that a piece would do, and the benefit that might come by the same, they became mad, as it were, after them, and would not stick to give any price they could attain to for them; accounting their bows and arrows but baubles in comparison of them.

The neighboring plantations resolved "to write to him, and in a friendly and neighborly way to admonish him to forbear these courses . . ." But, "he was so high as he scorned all advice and asked who had to do with him; he had and would trade pieces with the Indians in despite of all, with many other scurrilous terms full of disdain."

They sent to him a second time, and bade him be better advised and more temperate in his terms, for the country could not bear the injury he did; it was against their common safety, and against the king's proclamation. He answered in high terms as before and that the king's proclamation was no law; demanding what penalty was upon it. It was answered, more than he could bear, his majesty's displeasure. But insolently he persisted, and said the king was dead and his displeasure with him, and many the like things and threatened withal that if any came to molest him, let them look to themselves, for he would prepare for them.

They say "there was no way but to take him by force," and the Governor of Plymouth sent Captain Standish and some other aide with him. Morton's defense of Merrymount was something less than heroic.

They found him to stand stiffly in his defense, having made fast his doors, armed his consorts, set divers dishes of powder and bullets ready on the table; and if they had not been overarmed with drink, more hurt might have been done. They summoned him to yield, but he kept his house, and they could get nothing but scoffs and scorns from him; but at length, fearing they would do some violence to the house, he and some of his crew came out, but not to yield, but to shoot; but they were so steeled with drink as their pieces were too heavy for them; himself with a carbine (overcharged and almost half-filled with powder and shot, as was after found) had thought to have shot Captain Standish; but as he stepped to him, and put by his piece, land took him. Neither was there any hurt done to any of either side, save that one was so drunk that he ran his own nose upon the point of a sword that one held before him as he entered the house, but he lost but a little of his hot blood. Morton they brought away to Plymouth, where he was kept, till a ship went from the Isle of Shoals for England . . .

As Uncle Sam used to say, "The better the dancer the worse the man."

THE NAMING OF "BOSTON"

In the seventh century, a Roman Catholic monk by the name of Botolph, or Bot-holp, i.e., Boat-help, founded a church in what is now Lincolnshire, England. Gradually a town grew up around the church, and it was called Botolphstown, which was afterward contracted into Botolphston, and then shortened to Botoston, and finally Boston. From that town of Boston in Lincolnshire came to America the Rev. John Cotton, who gave the name to the New England capital.

WHY PENNSYLVANIA WAS SETTLED

Penn refused to pull his hat off
Before the king, and therefore sat off,
Another country to light pat on
Where he might worship with his hat on.

A PORTRAIT IN PERSPECTIVE:
MILES STANDISH

Miles Standish was essentially a man of action, better able than most to translate his intentions into deeds. Aside from the state into which the fair sex was able to reduce him (although at the time of the wooing of Priscilla Mullins, as described in Henry Wadsworth Longfellow's poem, "The Courtship of Miles Standish," he was but recently a widower), he was a fearless and ruthless man—one of the most intrepid of the soldiers of fortune so numerous in the seventeenth century.

Standish's reputation for action led the Pilgrims starting for the New World on the *Mayflower* in 1620 to hire him as their military protector. Truth to tell, Captain John Smith, who had mapped the entire coastline from Massachusetts to Maine, would have liked to accompany this party as its military leader. The frugal Pilgrims decided his price was too high, and Captain Smith was chagrined to find they were going to take his maps and charts instead of him. In his place they took the good right arm of Captain Standish, an English Catholic who had been a professional soldier on the Continent for many years, and his title, when he sailed on the *Mayflower*, was "Captain Miles Standish, Military Defender."

Captain Standish's method of dealing with the Indians was simple and direct. If they were friendly, he had nothing to do with them, for in such case Governor Bradford, the head of the colony, could negotiate with them through Tisquantum, who was one of the Indians who had been brought back to England by Captain Gosnold in 1602 as an exhibit for Queen Elizabeth's court. Due to his native intelligence, Tisquantum had not only become an immediate favorite with the English but also had acquired a good command of their language. He had returned to live with his tribe after debarking from the *Mayflower* and continued to act as an interpreter for the colonists. His efforts had much to do with their continued existence.

Standish's principle for dealing with enemy Indians was "kill before you are killed and fight to win." This was a soldier's credo. In later days, Boone and the other hunters and explorers had to live by the same law. To the Pilgrims, Captain Standish's actions were sanctioned by the harsh though just philosophy of the Old Testament: "An eye for an eye, a tooth for a tooth."

Captain Standish found a friendly advocate for the Pilgrims in the great chief, Massasoit. He found others warlike and hostile, particularly a chief named Caunbitant. Perhaps not so much out of meanness, but due to the fact that a group of white settlers had demeaned themselves by begging, and had deceived him by going back on their word, Caunbitant considered the white men interlopers and enemies. A match for Standish in character, Caunbitant's ambition was to drive the new arrivals from his land.

It is in dealing with this chief and others like him, implacable in warfare, that we find the least-known side of Captain Standish revealed. It is in the moment of crisis that men reveal themselves, and in his role as military defender Captain Standish encountered nothing but crises.

Let us, in this day of the motion picture, unreel a picture which we might call "The Life and Times of Captain Miles Standish in the Colonies." For a while, let us study him at two or three points in his career, under circumstances other than wife-seeking. An unfamiliar but nonetheless interesting figure emerges. As they say in Hollywood, let us look at the "rushes" on three separate "takes."

Miles Standish was a short man. This may explain some diffidence in his courting of Priscilla. It may also explain to the satisfaction of psychologists his ruthlessly offensive fighting. His attitude was the forerunner of what we have come to recognize—after studying the behavior of the Napoleon who functioned two centuries later—as the Napoleonic complex.

We are now ready for "take" Number One:

Caunbitant was the enemy not only of the colonists but also of Massasoit. The terrible winter of 1620 had reduced the number of English colonists by half, and Caunbitant plotted to wipe out the remainder completely before the next winter. His first step on this road was to capture Tisquantum and give out the news to the English that he was dead. The folks at Plymouth, who not only depended upon Tisquantum for services but who also were extremely devoted to him, immediately sent Captain Miles Standish and ten men to avenge his death. Because the Indians were contemptuous of the English habit of fighting in great numbers and also because he knew the savages were in no little awe of him personally, Standish took only ten men with him. Standish was also to discover the unknown fate of their friend Massasoit who had disappeared.

After a trip of several days, Standish and his little band arrived in the area where they believed Caunbitant had his headquarters. Before approaching the Indians, they sat down and ate from their knapsacks and then buried all of their equipment except that which was essential to fighting and existence. On entering the house where Caunbitant lived, they found an assemblage of Indians—men, women and children. At the sudden appearance of the Englishmen, there was much running to and fro, guns were unexpectedly fired, and many of the Indians went out a side door and escaped.

The English fell upon those who remained and beat them with rifle butts. Two bullets were fired by Standish's men but did not cause death. Standish was particularly courteous to the squaws, assuring them that he intended them no harm. Hearing this, the Indian children cried out, "Neensquaes! Neensquaes!" By this, they were saying, "I am a squaw! I am a squaw!"

From the squaws, Standish learned that Tisquantum had not been killed but was being held in their village and that Caunbitant had gone. Searching the other Indian houses, Standish found Tisquantum and released him. He and his little group of men left as they had come, taking Tisquantum with them.

We are now ready for "take" Number Two:

On his return, Captain Standish was met by another crisis. Certain of the Massachusetts Indians had become very bold and insulting. There was a simple explanation. The white men had lost face the preceding winter when some of the colonists, on the point of perishing from starvation and cold, had been forced to sell most of their clothes for food. They could not endure the rigors of the forest by reason of their nakedness. It was suggested that Standish take part of his men and investigate the situation. He, therefore, sent two of his men on to the Pilgrim colony with Tisquantum and proceeded himself to Wessaguschs, an outlying settlement of the Plymouth colony.

Standish found the people there going about their ordinary affairs. They refused to believe they were in danger of their lives. Standish told them of his knowledge that a plot against their existence was in progress. His idea was to assemble the ringleaders of the plot and execute them before they could attack, but the settlers would not hear of this. The presence of Standish did not produce fear in the Indians so much as it did antagonism. They sent him a message letting him know they understood the purpose of his visit. One of the Indian subchiefs, named Peksuot, sent this message, "Tell him we know he has come to kill us but we will not shun him. Let him begin when he dares to kill us but he will not take us unawares." Standish, however, did just that.

After considerable maneuvering, he managed on some pretext to have assembled in one place several antagonistic Indian chiefs. When they were all assembled, Standish insisted that they leave all weapons outside and the Indians complied. No sooner had the parley gotten under way than Standish gave a command to his men. The doors were bolted and the Englishmen produced weapons from inside their shirts and sleeves. They proceeded to kill all the Indians in the room with the exception of one eighteen-year-old boy who escaped. Standish pursued him, however, took him prisoner, and later had him hanged.

Now let us have "take" Number Three:

An interpreter named Hobbamock had accompanied Standish during all of this and congratulated the Englishman at the end of the massacre. He said to the captain, "Yesterday Peksuot bragged of his own strength and stature. He said though you were a great captain yet you were but a little man. Today I see you are big enough to lay him on the ground."

The few Indians who had escaped were pursued by Standish and his men. The arm of one of the savages had been broken by a chance shot and he capitulated. The rest of the Indians who escaped—some four in number—got into a swamp where they were forced to remain as long as Standish was in the area. For this massacre of the Indians he was officially reprimanded but secretly congratulated by the authorities. Exploits such as this made the Indians fear and respect Standish all the more and did much toward keeping their hostile activities in check.

This incident was only one example of Standish's treatment of the Indians. It was not only his hardness and thoroughness in dealing with any sign of hostility but also his luck that was to his credit. For example, on a night when he had intended sleeping alone by the banks of the Charles, a group of Indians decided to kill him. Their chosen executioner would have been able to carry out his mission had he succeeded in finding Standish. Truth to tell, the extreme cold of the night kept him from sleeping and so he was awake and alert when the assassins entered his room. After a hand-to-hand battle in which Standish killed seven Indians, the savages retreated.

Well, that was Captain Miles Standish, defender of the Plymouth colony. He did not remain in this role for he went back to England. However, the new land had become a part of him, and he returned to Plymouth colony where he was for a time treasurer and then assistant governor of the colony. He repeated his role of defender for many of the other New England colonies and finally retired to Duxbury, Massachusetts, where he died at the ripe old age of seventy-two.

After relating the speak-for-yourself-John story, Uncle Sam drew slowly on his pipe, and said, "Miles Standish was no pantywaist—without him as their leader the Pilgrims would have perished. They were peaceful men." He was silent a moment. "An army of stags led by a lion is more formidable than an army of lions led by a stag."

ON EXCESSIVE CHURCHGOING

It is difficult to bring a really good meeting to a close—the wives of Masons, Elks, and Woodsmen-of-the-World can attest this. This condition also prevailed in the year 1639; for example, look at the report of Governor John Winthrop of the Massachusetts Bay Colony in his diary:

December 3: There were so many lectures now in the country, and many poor persons would usually resort to two or three in the week, to the great neglect of their affairs, and the damage of the public. The assemblies also were [in divers churches] held till night, and sometimes within the night, so as such as dwelt far off could not get home in due season, and many weak bodies could not endure so long, in the extremity of the heat or cold, without great trouble, and hazard of their health.

Objections were actually made to the civil authorities and the General Court ordered the elders of the church to "give a meeting to the magistrates and deputies, to consider about the length and frequency of church assemblies" and report to the court. This was taken in ill part by most of the elders and others of the churches, "they alleging their tenderness of the church's liberties, that this order might enthrall them to the civil power, and cast a blemish upon the elders, which would remain to

41

posterity, that they should needs to be regulated by the civil magistrates, and also raise an ill savor of the people's coldness, that would complain of much preaching," etc. Further, to listen to preaching the way they wanted it was "the main end of our coming hither."

To this Winthrop writes, the Court answered:

December 3: 1. That the order was framed with as much tenderness and respect as might be in general words, without mentioning sermons or lectures, so as it might as well be taken for meetings upon other occasions of the churches, which were known to be very frequent.

2. It carried no command, but only an expression of a desire.

3. It concluded nothing, but only to confer and consider.

4. The record of such an order will be rather an argument of the zeal and forwardness of the elders and churches, as it was of the Israelites, when they offered so liberally to the service of the tabernacle, as Moses was forced to restrain them.

The magistrates finally were satisfied with an agreement by the churches "That their church assemblies might ordinarily break up in such session, as people that dwell a mile or two off might get home by daylight."

THE CROSS-EXAMINATION
OF A WITCH

A religious hysteria swept Salem, Massachusetts, in 1692. People accused each other indiscriminately, without foundation in most instances, and the accused were always forced to defend themselves publicly before a court. The trials were brought to a close when the accusations turned against the judges themselves, the accused becoming accusers in self-defense. So far as is known, nineteen persons were hanged and one man was killed.

One Sarah Good, the wife of William Good of Salem Village, was brought into court on March 1, 1692, charged with having "Wickedly and feloniously . . . used, Practised and Exorcised . . . certain Detestable arts called Witchcrafts and Sorceries."

Here is the cross-examination of Sarah Good before the worshipful Examiners John Harthorn and Jonathan Curran:

Q. Sarah Good, what evil Spirit have you familiarity with?
A. None.
Q. Have you made no contracts with the devil?
A. No.
Q. Why doe you hurt these children?
A. I doe not hurt them. I scorn it.
Q. Who doe you imploy then to doe it?

43

A. I imploy no body.

Q. What creature do you imploy then?

A. No creature but I am falsely accused.

Q. Why did you go away muttering from Mr. Parris his house?

A. I did not mutter but I thanked him for what he gave my child.

Q. Have you made no contract with the devil?

A. No.

We desired the children all of them to look upon her and see if this were the person that had hurt them and so they all did looke upon her, and said this was one of the persons that did torment them—presently they were all tormented.

Q. Sarah Good, do you not see how what you have done, why doe you not tell us the truth, why doe you thus torment these poor children?

A. I doe not torment them.

Q. Who doe you imploy then?

A. I imploy nobody. I scorn it.

Q. How came they thus tormented?

A. What doe I know; you bring others here and now you charge me with it.

Q. Why who was it?

A. I doe not know but it was some you brought into the meeting house with you.

Q. Wee brought you into the meeting house.

A. But you brought in two more.

Q. Who was it then that tormented the children?

A. It was Osburn.

Q. What is it you say when you go muttering away from persons' houses?

A. If I must tell I will tell.

Q. Doe tell us then.

A. If I must tell, I will tell, it is the commandments. I may say my commandments I hope.

Q. What commandment is it? ·

A. If I must tell, I will tell, it is a psalm.

Q. What psalm?

A. (After a long time she muttered over some part of a psalm.)

Q. Who doe you serve?

A. I serve God.

Q. What God doe you serve?

A. The God that made heaven and earth.

(Though shee was not willing to mention the word God. Her answers were in a very wicked spitfull manner, reflecting and retorting against the authority with base and abussive words and many lies shee was taken in. . . .)

"Many a simple man and woman hides his or her light under a bushel of ignorance," Dr. Sam said to me, speaking from a lifetime of human encounters. "Faith and ignorance are matters which should not be pried out of anyone."

He then quoted Daniel Webster's speech in New York in 1831: "There is no happiness. There is no liberty. There is no enjoyment of life unless a man can say, when he rises in the morning, 'I shall be subject to the decision of no unwise judge today.'"

FREEDOM IS RELATIVE

It seems to be an historical truism that a fanatic minority desiring freedom to worship will as often refuse freedom to a group with whom they disagree. When the Boston divines discovered that William Penn, the Quaker, had been given land in America, they were greatly upset. Cotton Mather wrote in "September ye 15th, 1682,"

There bee now at sea a shippe (for our friend, Mr. Esaias Holcraft, of London, did advise me by ye last packet that it wolde sail some time in August) called ye *Welcome*, R. Greenaway, master, which has aboard an hundred or more of ye heretics and malignants called Quakers, with W. Penne, who is ye chief scampe at ye hedde of them. Ye General Court has accordingly given secret orders to Master Malachi Hexett, of ye brig Porposse, to waylaye ye said *Welcome* as near the coast of Codde as may be, and make captive ye said Penne and his ungodlie crew, so that ye Lord may be glorified and not mocked on ye soil of this new countrie with ye heathen worshippe of these people. Much spoyl can be made by selling ye whole lotte to Barbadoes, where slaves fetch good prices in rumme and sugar, and we shall not only do ye Lord great service by punishing ye wicked, but shall make great gayne for his ministers

46

and people. Master Huxett feels hopeful, and I will set down ye news he brings when his shippe comes back.

   Yours in ye bowels of Christ,
                    Cotton Mather

"So much for religious tolerance," said Dr. Sam.

HOW WOMEN SHOULD ACT

"Bluestockings," intellectual women, were not unknown in colonial days. In Boston, which quickly lost the aspect of a frontier town, a literary life was possible for the female, one that was not too different from that of a lady of ease in any European city.

Mrs. Anne Bradstreet, wife of Simon Bradstreet, Governor of Plymouth Colony in 1630, was known for her poetry, wit, and learning. John Norton, in a poetical description of her character, wrote:

> Her breast was a brave palace, a broad street,
> Where all heroic, ample thoughts did meet,
> Where nature such a tenement had tane,
> What other souls to hers dwelt in a lane!

However, not all men believed in a woman's even knowing how to read and write. "Ever flatten a cat's ears with your hand? You get a kind of furry malignity! Same with women in bloomers!" said Dr. Sam who got along with Carrie Nation about as well as a bull moose with a lady preacher. "A she who's pelt has ris' above her eyebrow is a highbrow!"

General John Winthrop wrote an essay in 1645, "Objections to Women's Education," on the occasion of the Governor of Connecticut bringing his wife to Boston to be treated:

Mr. Hopkins, the Governor of Hartford upon Connecticut came to Boston and brought his wife with him (a Godly young woman, and of special parts) who has fallen into a sad infirmity, the loss of her understanding and reason, which had been growing upon her divers years, by occasions of her giving herself wholly to reading and writing, and she had written many books.

Her husband, being very loving and tender of her, was loath to grieve her, but he saw his error when it was too late. For if she had attended to her household affairs, and such things as belong to women, and had not gone out of her way to meddle in such things as are proper for men, whose minds are stronger &c., she had kept her wits and might have improved them usefully and honorably in the place God had set her.

When I think of how women have changed I am reminded of Matthew Arnold's warning, "Change doth unknit the tranquil strength of men."

WOMEN'S CLOTHES

My Lady Greensleeves in England dressed elegantly. Con-
temporaneously, a popular ballad of the day went into detail on
the elements of dress. The ardent swain of the song enumer-
ates:

> I have been readie at your hand,
> To grant whatever you would crave,
> I have both waged life and land,
> Your love and good will for to have.
>
> I bought thee kerchers to thy head,
> That were wrought fine and gallantly;
> I kept thee both at board and bed,
> Which cost my purse well favouredly.
>
> Thy girdle of gold so red,
> With pearls bedecked sumptuously;
> The like no other lasses had,
> And yet thou wouldst not love me.
>
> Thy crimson stockings all of silk,
> With golde all wrought above the knee,
> Thy pumps as white as was the milk,
> And yet thou wouldst not love me.

Thy gown was of the grossie green,
Thy sleeves of satten hanging by,
Which made thee be our harvest queen,
And yet thou wouldst not love me.

And for the record, it is well to note this faithful swain presented his coy mistress with other services:

My gayest gelding I thee gave,
To ride wherever liked thee.
No ladie ever was so brave,
And yet thou wouldst not love me.

My men were clothèd all in green,
And they did ever wait on thee;
All this was gallant to be seen,
And yet thou wouldst not love me.

They set thee up, they took thee downe,
They served thee with humilitie,
Thy foote might not once touch the ground,
And yet thou wouldst not love me.

For everie morning when thou rose,
I sent thee dainties orderly;
To cheare thy stomack from all woes,
And yet thou wouldst not love me.

And who did pay for all this geare,
That thou didst spend when pleased thee?
Even I that am rejected here,
And thou did dainst to love me.

Of women's clothes in the colonies, Nathaniel Ward wrote in the mid-seventeenth century: "To speak moderately, I truly confess it is beyond the ken of my understanding to conceive how those women should have any true grace or valuable virtue that have so little wit as to disfigure themselves with such exotic garb, as not only dismantles their native lovely lustre but trans-clouts them into gantbar-geese, ill-shapen-shotten shellfish, Egyptian hieroglyphics, or at the best into French flirts of the pantry, which a proper English woman should scorn with her heels."

"In the days when a lady's bustle was known as a 'bishop,' " said Dr. Sam as we watched the pretty girls go by in their cotton dresses one summer afternoon in New York City, "they really strutted at the Sunday prayer meetings! 'If, by her "bishop" or her "grace" alone, a genuine lady or a church is known,' " he quoted his ancestor, adding a little of his own afterthoughts, "think of the rough diamonds passed off as glass, and vice versa . . . aye, that's the way of a verse about vice."

In 1817, when straw bonnets first came into general use, it was common to trim them with artificial wheat or barley, in ears; whence the following:

> Who now of threatening famine dare complain,
> When every female forehead teems with grain?
> See how the wheat-sheaves nod amid the plumes:
> Our barns are now transferred to drawing-rooms,
> And husbands who indulge in active lives,
> To fill their granaries, may thresh their wives!

Dr. Sam had a song for the woman "clothes horse":

> I don't like to see women wear satin for dresses
> Their husbands at home wrapped up in distresses;
> They'd better be at home a-washing their dishes
> And likewise a-mending their husband's old britches.

WELSH INDIANS?

Here is a mystery.

A Welsh clergyman, traveling on the James River, was frightened to see Indians on the bank, keeping pace with the shallop in which he and three companions were en route to Jamestown. When the banks of the river narrowed, the Indians waded out and before they could be fired upon, overturned the boat and captured the travelers. The clergyman, a Welshman, prayed in his own language.

There was great excitement! The Indians surrounded the clergyman. He expected immediate death, but they raised him to his feet and jabbered to him. He found that he understood them! Their speech was a dialect of Welsh!

The Indians killed his companions but kept the Welshman prisoner. At the Indian village, he found the Indian language little different from his own. Then the Indians showed him a Bible, which they could not read. They asked him to read it to them. He found it was a twelfth century Welsh Bible! How they had it, they did not know. They said it had been in their tribe for many generations.

The clergyman was released and returned to England planning to return and Christianize the Welsh-speaking Indians. He died before doing so and nothing further was heard of them until 1782. That year, Captain Isaac Stuart, of the Provincial

Cavalry of South Carolina, wrote the following narrative, which we find in the South Carolina archives:

I was taken prisoner, about 50 miles to the westward of Fort Pitt, about 18 years ago, by the Indians, and carried to the Wabash, with other white men. They were executed, with circumstances of horrid barbarity; but it was my good fortune to call forth the sympathy of a good woman of the village, who was permitted to redeem me from those who held me prisoner, by giving them a horse as a ransom. After remaining two years in bondage, a Spaniard came to the nation, having been sent from Mexico on discoveries. He made application to the chiefs of the Indians for hiring me, and another white man who was in the like situation, a native of Wales, and named John Davey, which was complied with. We took our departure and travelled to the westward, crossing the Mississippi near Red River, up which we travelled upwards of 700 miles. Here we came to a nation of Indians remarkably white, and whose hair was of a reddish color, at least, mostly so. They lived on a small river which emptied itself into Red River, which they called the River Post; and in the morning, the day after our arrival, the Welshman informed me that he was determined to remain with the nation of Indians, giving as a reason that he understood their language, it being very little different from the Welsh. My curiosity was excited very much by this information, and I went with my companion to the chief men of the town, who informed him, in a language that I had no knowledge of, and which had no affinity with that of any other Indian tongue that I ever heard, that the forefathers of this nation came from a foreign country, and landed on the east side of the Mississippi (describing particularly the country now called West Florida); and that, on the Spaniards taking possession of the country, they fled to their then abode; and, as a proof of what they advanced, they brought out rolls of parchment wrote with blue ink, at least it had a bluish cast. The characters I did not understand, and the Welshman being unacquainted with letters of any language, I was not able to know what the meaning of the writing was. They were a bold, hardy, intrepid people, very warlike, and their women were beautiful, compared with other Indians.

What is the answer to the mystery? One possible explanation comes from the Welsh. In 1570, a group of Welshmen sailed westward in ten ships and were never heard of again. Could they have reached the shores of America?

THE 'HOLY' TERROR OF CHILDREN

Colonial children, from the moment they could toddle, were taken to church with their elders. The hell-fire sermons to which they had to listen had a profound and lasting effect upon them. A Mr. Sewell's diary describes the effect of such a sermon on the mind of his young daughter, Betty:

A little while after dinner she burst out into an amazing cry, which caused all the family to cry too. Her mother asked her the reason; she gave none. At last she said she was afraid she should go to Hell; her sins were not pardoned. She was first wounded by my reading a sermon of Mr. Norton's Text, 'ye shall seek me and shall not find me.' And those words in the sermon, 'ye shall seek me and die in your sins,' ran in her mind and terrified her greatly. She told me she was afraid she should go to Hell. . . .

Uncle Sam often shook his head on the actions of people to people, "Man is not so soon healed as hurt."

A LOCAL CELEBRATION
IN THE SOUTH

Not long ago I was walking down the street of Shreveport, Louisiana, with a southern gentleman of that city. I remarked on the goodly number of pretty girls adorning the streets of his fair city and he replied, "There are no more pretty women in the South than up North. It's just that we have more time to look at them."

Well, this is very revealing about the attitude of the South, not only as it is now but as it was in colonial days, for in the colonial South the diversions of Merrie England were not neglected as they were in diligent New England. An account in the *Virginia Gazette* of Hanover County lists the following coming events:

We have advice from Hanover County, that on St. Andrew's Day there are to be Horse Races and several other Diversions, for the entertainment of the Gentlemen and Ladies, at the Old Field, near Captain John Bickerton's in that county (if permitted by the Hon. Wm. Byrd, Esquire, Proprietor of said land), the substance of which is as follows, viz:

(1) It is proposed that 20 Horses and Mares do run around a three miles' course for a prize of five pounds.

(2) That a hat of the value of 20 c. be cudgelled for, and

that after the first challenge made the Drums are to beat every quarter of an hour for three challenges round the Ring, and none to play with their Left hand.

(3) That a violin be played for by 20 Fiddlers; no person to have the liberty of playing unless he brings a fiddle with him. After the prize is won they are all to play together, and each a different tune, to be treated by the Company.

(4) That 12 boys of 12 years of age do run 112 yards for a Hat of the cost of 12 shillings.

(5) That a handsome entertainment be provided for the subscribers and their wives; and such of them as are not so happy as to have wives may treat any other lady.

(6) That Drums, Trumpets, Hautboys, &c., be provided to play at said entertainment.

(7) That after dinner the Royal Health, His Honor the Governor's, &c., are to be drunk.

(8) That a Quire of ballads be sung for by a number of Songsters, all of them to have liquor sufficient to clear their Wind Pipes . . .

(9) That a pair of handsome Silk Stockings of one Pistole value be given to the handsomest young country maid that appears in the Field.

With many other Whimsical and Comical Diversions too numerous to mention.

The account ends on a slightly less exhilarating note:

And as this mirth is designed to be purely innocent and void of offence, all persons resorting there are desired to have themselves with decency and sobriety; the subscribers being resolved to discountenance all immorality with the utmost rigor.

SOME EARLY COLONIAL EPITAPHS

In colonial days most epitaphs were sentimental and praised the deceased. Benjamin Franklin wrote in *Poor Richard's Almanac,* "Here comes glib tongue; who can out-flatter a dedication, and be like ten epitaphs."

However, humor was present.

In memoriam of John Foster, who set up the first printing press in Boston and who died in 1681:

> Thy body, which no activeness did lack,
> Now's laid aside like an old almanac,
> But for the present only's out of date;
> 'Twill have at length a far more active state.
> Yea, though with dust thy body soilèd be,
> Yet at the resurrection we shall see
> A fair edition, and of matchless worth,
> Free from errata, new in Heaven set forth;
> 'Tis but a word from God, the great Creator—
> It shall be done when he saith Imprimatur.

I who was once called Peter (a stone), am now covered by a stone (petra); and I who was once named Comestor (devourer), am now devoured. I taught when alive, nor do I cease to teach, though dead; for he who beholds me reduced to ashes may say,—"This man was once what we are now; and what he is now, we soon shall be."

AT OXFORD, NEW HAMPSHIRE

To all my friends I bid adieu,
  A more sudden death you never knew,
As I was leading the old mare to drink
  She kicked, and killed me quicker'n a wink.

FROM AN EARLY GRAVESTONE IN ESSEX, MASS.

Here lies the man Richard,
  And Mary his wife,
Whose surname was Pritchard:
  They lived without strife;
And the reason was plain,—
  They abounded in riches,
They had no care nor pain,
  And his wife wore the breeches.

In Dorchester, Mass., is the epitaph on a young woman:

On the 21st of March
God's angels made a sarche.
Around the door they stood;
They took a maid,
It is said,
And cut her down like wood.

When I was born I cried, while others smiled;
Oh, may I dying smile, while others weep.

I came in the morning,—it was spring,
    And I smiled;
I walked out at noon,—it was summer,
    And I was glad;
I sat me down at even,—it was autumn,
    And I was sad;
I laid me down at night,—it was winter,
    And I slept.

She who lies beneath this stone
Died of constancy alone;
Fear not to approach, oh, passer-by—
Of naught contagious did she die.

As Will Rogers said, "Everything is funny as long as it happens to somebody else."

THE WHITE WOMAN WHO
SCALPED THE INDIANS

Outside of Boston and the coast settlements, women found the Indians a constant danger in all new outposts. There were many instances of friendliness but more of attacks. A description of one such affair from Cotton Mather's *Magnalia Christi Americana* is extremely dramatic:

On the 15th of March 1697, a band of about twenty Indians came unexpectedly upon Haverhill in Massachusetts. The house which this party of Indians singled out as their object of attack belonged to Thomas Dunstan. Alarmed by the shouts of the Indians, he had only time to direct his children's flight (seven in number) the extremes of whose ages were 2 and 17 and the Indians were upon them. His wife who but a week before had been confirmed by a child was unable to arise from her bed to the distraction of her agonized husband. Mr. Dunstan was forced to follow his children in order to protect them. By a miracle none of the little retreating party were hurt. The Indians did not pursue long for fear of raising the neighboring English. Hence, this part of the family escaped to place of safety.

The Indians were now in undisturbed possession of the house and having driven the sick woman from her bed, compelled her to sit quietly in the corner of the fireplace, while they completed the pillage of the house. This business was being finished, it was set on fire, and Mrs. Dunstan, who before considered herself unable to walk, was, at the approach of night obliged to march into the wilderness and take her bed upon the cold ground. Mrs. Neff, a widow, who had stayed behind to share her fate attempted to escape with the infant child. She was intercepted, the child taken from her, and its brains beat out against a neighboring apple tree. Mrs. Neff was compelled to accompany her new and frightful masters. The captives amounted in all to thirteen, some of whome, as they became unable to travel, were murdered and left exposed upon the way.

The final fate of Mrs. Dunstan and her Indian captors is most unusual. Mrs. Dunstan became famous as "the woman who scalped the Indians."

After two days' journey Mary Dunstan found herself stronger. The captives were divided among the Indian families to work as slaves. Mrs. Dunstan and Mrs. Neff and a boy named Samuel Leonardson were given to an Indian family of twelve persons; two men, three women and seven children. This family was comparatively kind to the prisoners, feeding and clothing them although forcing them to backbreaking work.

One of the Indian women told Mary Dunstan that on reaching the Indian village, she and the others would be forced to run the gantlet. Few survived this Indian martyrdom and these few were often crippled. Mary determined that given an opportunity she would try to save herself and the others. Perhaps she could kill her captors.

This was a feat that might possibly be accomplished. The Indian family and the three prisoners were traveling separately from the main body of the tribe. Mary discussed it first with Mrs. Neff and then with the English boy, both of whom agreed the alternative was their own death.

One night, while the others slept, Mary Dunstan decided what should be done. In the morning she instructed the English boy, who had won the Indians' confidence, to find out how to scalp! Mrs. Dunstan, being a very practical woman, also thought that they could turn their escape to some practical end if they were lucky. After all, she reasoned, there was a bounty given to every settler who brought in evidence of having killed an Indian. Since the Indian men had made a mascot of the boy and were instructing him in woodlore, they told him about scalping without suspicion. By this time the prisoners had been on the march for two weeks.

It was a comparatively mild night, and the Indians fell into a sound sleep. Mrs. Dunstan awakened her fellow captives, and armed herself and the boy with their captors' tomahawks. Mrs. Neff could not bring herself to take part in the slaughter. Allocating two Indian men and two women to herself, Mrs. Dunstan assigned one of the women and the children to the boy. So truly did they direct their blows that only one of the women escaped death. She was so badly wounded that she could not act against them. The youngest boy, who had befriended the English lad, was allowed to escape. By dawn Mary Dunstan had ten scalps in her hand and was ready to leave.

To prevent pursuit, Mary had her companions scuttle all but one of the Indians' canoes. With the provisions and arms of their victims, the three embarked on the river and followed the Merrimac downstream. The trip took a week but they all arrived at their homes without incident.

Mrs. Dunstan demanded, and received, the homage of a heroine. Her story was carried in all the newspapers of the day. The ten scalps were evidence not to be questioned, and the General Court awarded her and the English boy fifty pounds. Numerous other gifts came to her from other sources. So far as we know, she returned to the site of her burned home, which her husband rebuilt, and lived there until a ripe old age, retelling this same story to all who might care to listen.

"She showed great presence of mind," said my grandmother.
". . . the next best thing to absence of body!" Dr. Sam said disapprovingly.

ALCOHOLISM AND THE INDIANS

From the very beginning, we find it was the custom of the settlers to give the Indians strong liquor. "They wanted the Indians to be on a virtual 'alcoholiday,' " said Dr. Sam.

The Indian chiefs realized how disintegrating liquor's effect on their people was, but they could not prevent them from buying it or the settlers from selling it. Mr. Thomas Budd, in *Good Order Established, a Report published in 1678*, quotes from the speech of one Indian chief as follows:

The strong liquor was first sold to us by the Dutch; and they were blind, they had no eyes, they did not see that it was for our hurt; the next people that came among us were the Swedes, who continued the sale of those strong liquors to us; they were also blind, they had no eyes, they did not see it to be hurtful to us to drink it, although we know it to be hurtful to us; but if people will sell it to us, we are so in love with it that we cannot forbear it; when we drink it, it makes us mad, we do not know what to do, we then abuse one another, we throw each other into the fire. Seven score of our people have been killed by reason of drinking it, since the time it was first sold to us: Those people that sell it are blind, they have no eyes; but now there is a people come to live among us, they have eyes, they see it to be for our hurt, and we know it to be for our hurt: they are willing to deny themselves the profit of it for our good: these people have eyes: we are glad such a people are come amongst us: we must put it down by mutual consent: the cask must be sealed up: it must be made fast, it must not leak by day nor by night, in the light nor in the dark: and we give you these four belts of wampum, which we would have you lay up safe, and keep by you, to be witnesses of this agreement that we make with you: and we would have you tell your children, that these four belts of wampum are given you to be witnesses betwixt us and you of this agreement.

Speaking of strong drink, Uncle used to say, "My boy, beware of a drinking companion with a memory."

WEATHER SUPERSTITIONS

Current in England and the Colonies in the seventeenth century were the Shepherd's Calendars that explained certain signs by which the weather could be forecast. Considering our dissatisfaction with scientific weather bureaus and the reports of the daily newspapers, perhaps it would be well for us to memorize the portents as described below:

The behavior of birds:
Sea and fresh-water fowls such as cormorants, sea gulls, moor hens, etc., flying from sea to land.
Land fowls chasing, washing, and noisy in the evening, flying to water.
Geese, ducks, coots, etc., pecking, shaking, washing and noisy.
Rooks and crows in flocks suddenly disappearing.
The raven crying in the morning with an interruption in its notes.
Crows being very clamorous at evening.
The bittern and swallow flying low.
Poultry going to rest early.
Tame fowls grubbing in the dust and clapping their wings.
Peacocks and owls unusually clamorous.
The late- and early-crowing cock clapping his wings.

The behavior of beasts:
Oxen snuffing the air, looking to the south, while lying on their sides.
Calves running violently and gamboling.
Cats washing their faces and ears.
Foxes barking.
A grumbling noise in the belly of a hound.
Cattle gasping for air at noon.

The behavior of insects:
Worms crawling in superabundance.
Ants hastening into their nests.
Bees keeping close to their hives.
Frogs drawing nigh to houses for their croaking.
Gnats singing more than usual.

Dr. Sam never talked about the weather. Once, when I asked him why, he answered, "Sonny, there are only two kinds of weather—bad and unusual. Why talk about 'em?" Thereupon he paradoxically launched into his "Memphis Annie," the weather rhymes of the months of the year:

January snowy,	July moppy,
February flowy,	August croppy,
March blowy,	September poppy,
April showery,	October breezy,
May flowery,	November wheezy,
June bowery,	December freezy.

"Learned men make calendars . . . but God makes the weather," Uncle Sam always said.

BROADSIDES

Puritans and other religious groups frowned upon songs on other than religious subjects. These religious groups sang only church music, although they did allow semireligious folk songs as a part of the observance of holidays.

In Massachusetts, the identification of church with state excluded the singing of ballads and secular songs. However, ballads were present. Cotton Mather inveighed against "foolish songs and ballads" which hawkers and peddlers carried from one colony to another. In the middle and southern colonies, where the religious tradition was less rigid, old English broadsides, popular ballads and songs were sung along with the religious and semireligious songs.

In the South, as well as in New York and Pennsylvania, ballads were sung, broadsides were sold, and there was singing in the taverns. Madrigals were, of course, offered in the drawing rooms and brought over from England.

When we listen to the music from this era that is still living and sung in various parts of the United States—the folk music of the United States—we find that the old songs from Great Britain still retain their strength and beauty. We find that the old melodies with new words become the source of songs up to the very present. However, don't assume that all the songs were brought across the ocean. The settlers were a virile and creative people and as early as 1630 we find broadsides and songs that referred to events happening in the Colonies. Throughout the Colonies, broadsides in meter were published that announced events and took the place of newspapers. Their role in transmitting news cannot be underestimated. Nor should their effectiveness as propaganda. Take, for example, the one of "Captain Kidd." Inevitably, the metered accounts had traditional tunes to which they could be sung.

Captain Kidd was not a pirate at all but an exceptionally unsuccessful privateer. Captain Kidd of New York was put in charge of a thirty-gun ship, *The Adventure Galley*. The governors of New York, Massachusetts, and New Hampshire, the King himself, and several other noted figures formed a stock company and sent *The Adventure Galley* to hunt out and destroy pirates. *The Adventure Galley* found no pirates but did attack, and quite legally, ships flying the colors of France and India.

Unfortunately, Captain Kidd's existence became politically inconvenient to King William and the other sponsors when there was a temporary truce between England and France. Kidd had hit a mutinous gunner, William Moore, on the head with a wooden bucket, resulting in his death. On this excuse he was arrested, convicted and sent to the gallows in London. One of the first instances of deliberate propaganda, popular sentiment was directed against Kidd by a ballad purporting to tell his story. As a contemporary said, Captain Kidd was hanged "by a doggerel ballad sung to a villainous tune." The tune actually is quite memorable and several hymns have been written to its strain.

Oh, my name was William Kidd, as I sailed, as I sailed,
My name was William Kidd, as I sailed.
My name was William Kidd, God's laws I did forbid,
And most wickedly I did, as I sailed, as I sailed.

Oh, my parents taught me well, as I sailed, as I sailed,
My parents taught me well, as I sailed.

My parents taught me well, to shun the gates of hell,
But against them I rebelled, as I sailed, as I sailed.

Oh, I murdered William Moore, as I sailed, as I sailed,
I murdered William Moore, as I sailed.
I murdered William Moore, and left him in his gore,
Not many leagues from shore, as I sailed, as I sailed.

Oh, I steered from sound to sound, as I sailed, as I sailed,
I steered from sound to sound, as I sailed.
I steered from sound to sound, and many ships I found,
And all of them I burned, as I sailed, as I sailed.

And being cruèl still, as I sailed, as I sailed,
And being cruèl still, as I sailed.
And being cruèl still, my gunner I did kill,
And his precious blood did spill, as I sailed, as I sailed.

I was sick and nigh to death, as I sailed, as I sailed,
I was sick and nigh to death, as I sailed.
I was sick and nigh to death, and I vowed with every breath
To walk in wisdom's ways, when I sailed, when I sailed.

My repentance lasted not, as I sailed, as I sailed,
My repentance lasted not, as I sailed.
My repentance lasted not, my vows I soon forgot
Damnation was my lot, as I sailed, as I sailed.

To the execution dock I must go, I must go,
To the execution dock I must go.
To the execution dock, while many thousands flock,
But I must bear the shock and must die, and must die.

Take a warning now by me, for I must die, for I must die,
Take a warning now by me for I must die.
Take a warning now by me and shun bad company
Lest you come to hell with me, for I must die, I must die.

One of the most delightful news broadsides to come down to us is the story of Old John Webb's escape from prison. He was in prison with a youth known to us only as "John."

> There were nine to guard the British ranks
> And five to guard the town about,
> And two to stand at either hand,
> And one to let old Tenor out.

(Chorus)
> Billy broke locks, and Billy broke bolts,
> And Billy broke all that he came nigh,
> Until he came to the dungeon door,
> And that he broke right manfully.

> There was eighty weight of good Spanish iron
> Between his neck-bone and his knee,
> But Billy took Johnny up under his arm
> And lugged him away right artfully.

> They mounted their horse and away did ride
> (And who but they rode gallantly)
> Until they came to the river bank,
> And there they alighted right merrily.

> And then they called for a room to dance
> (And who but they danced merrily) ,
> And the best dancer among them all
> Was old John Webb who was just set free.

Benjamin Franklin writes in his Autobiography of being nine years old when:

My brother put me on composing occasional ballads. One was called "The Lighthouse Tragedy" . . . the other was a sailor's song on the taking of Teach (or Blackbeard the

72

Pirate). They were wretched stuff, in the grub street ballad style; and when they were printed he sent me about the town to sell them. The first sold wonderfully, the event being recent, having made a great noise.

But not all broadsides were of political news . . . there were the tabloid stories of unrequited love, murder . . . or indeed anything. Take the song that has become our earliest folk song. Mr. Timothy Myrick, son of Lt. Thomas Myrick of Springfield Mountain (now Wilbraham), Masschusetts, was bitten by a rattlesnake on Friday, August 7, 1761, at Farmington, Massachusetts, and died before he could reach home. He was twenty-two years, two months, and three days old, and "very near the point of marriage" to Sarah Blake. His gravestone is still in existence. The original broadside was an elegy over his tragic death, which may have been sung at his funeral to the tune of "Old Hundred" in accordance with a custom in western Massachusetts.

> On Springfield Mountain
>   There did dwell
> A love—lye youth,
>   I knowed him well.
>
> He scarce had mowed
>   Half round the field
> When an ug—lye serpent
>   Bit his heel.
>
> They took him home
>   To Mol—lye dear
> Which made her feel
>   So ve—rye queer.
>
> Now Mol—lye had
>   Two ruby lips

With which the pizen
She did sip.

Now Mol—lye had
A rotten tooth
And so the pizen
Killed them both.

This version is the one popularized by music halls of the early 1800's and is an example of how a broadside song can live many lives, until today our top singers do versions of it to a rock-and-roll rhythm.

Another song which has gone through the same series of changes is one that celebrated a murder that took place in 1810 in Pennsylvania. The victim's name was not Polly, but since "Pretty Polly" was the heroine of an old English murder ballad, the broadside, as we finally have it in hand, uses this name for the victim. No tabloid newspaper ever recounted a more gory crime.

He courted pretty Polly the live-long night,
Then left her next morning before it was light.

Pretty Polly, pretty Polly, come go along with me,
Before we get married some pleasures to see.

She jumped on behind him and away they did go,
Over the hills and the valley below.

They went a little further and what did they spy,
A new dug grave with a spade laying by.

O, Willie, oh, Willie, I'm 'fraid of your way;
I'm afraid you will lead my poor body astray.

Pretty Polly, pretty Polly, you've guessed about right,
For I slept on your grave the best part of last night.

He throwed her on the ground and she broke into tears,
She throwed her arms around him and trembled with fear.

There's no time to talk now, there's no time to stand,
He drew out his knife all in his right hand.

He stabbed her in the heart and the blood it did flow,
And into the grave pretty Polly did go.

He put on a little dirt and he started for home;
Leaving no one behind but the wild birds to moan.

A debt to the devil Willie must pay;
For killing pretty Polly and running away.

PREPARING DINNER FOR THE FAMILY:
1720

The housewife of 1720 could buy an interesting variety of
food for her family at interesting prices. In his description of
plantation life in Virginia, a Mr. Robert Beverly described the
following availabilities on the market. In reading his survey,
remember that one penny equals a little more than one cent and
a shilling equals about fourteen cents:

Their fish is in vast plenty and variety, and extraordinarily
good of its kind. Beef and pork are commonly sold there
at from one penny to two pence the pound, or more, according to the time of the year; their fattest and largest pullets
at six pence apiece; their chickens at three or four shillings
the dozen; their ducks at eight pence or nine pence apiece;
their geese at ten pence or a shilling; their turkey hens at
15 or 18 pence; their turkey cocks at two shillings or half
a crown. Oysters and wild fowl are not so dear as poultry,
and in their season are the cheapest food they have. Their
deer are commonly sold from five to 10 shillings according
to their scarcity or goodness.

THE AMERICAN NEGRO IN 1724

"A man for sale?" Dr. Sam, who hated any kind of kowtowing, raised and lowered his eyebrows furiously on reading the dispassionate manuscript of Mr. Hugh Jones, circa 1750. "Why, to hold a Man in print, requires a large M, just as . . ." The doctor hooked his thumbs in his ample belt. ". . . it requires a large belt to hold his potential. Yes, for any man, sir, a capital M is a must, and as my respected uncle used to say, 'you can't trade in capital, sir!' That would be adding 'insult to usury!' "

The negroes live in small cottages called quarters, in about six in a gang, under the direction of an overseer or bailiff; who takes care that they tend such land as the owner allots and orders, upon which they raise hogs and cattle, and plant Indian corn (or maize) and tobacco for the use of their master; out of which the overseer has a dividend (or share) in proportion to the number of hands including himself; this with several privileges in his salary, and is an ample recompense for his pains, and encouragement of his industrious care, as to the labour, health, and provision of the negroes. The negroes are very numerous, some gentlemen having hundreds of them of all sorts, to whom they bring great profit; for the sake of which they are obliged to keep them well, and not overwork, starve, or famish them, besides other inducements to favour them; which is done in a great degree, to such especially that are laborious, careful, and honest; though indeed some masters, careless of their own interest or reputation, are too cruel and negligent.

The negroes are not only increased by fresh supplies from Africa and the West India Islands, but also are very prolific among themselves; and they that are born there talk good English, and affect our language, habits, and customs; and though they be naturally of a barbarous and cruel temper, yet are they kept under by severe discipline upon occasion, and by good laws are prevented from running away, injuring their English, or neglecting their business.

Their work (or chimerical hard slavery) is not very laborious; their greatest hardship consisting in that they and their posterity are not at their own liberty or disposal, but are the property of their owners; and when they are free, they know not how to provide so well for themselves generally; neither did they live so plentifully nor (many of them) so easily in their own country, where they are made slaves to one another, or taken captive by their enemies.

The children belong to the master of the woman that bears them; and such as are born of a negro and an European are called mulattoes; but such as are born of an Indian and negro are called mustees.

AGGRANDIZEMENT: 1743

The importance of a title in the social scale and its use for personal aggrandizement and social furtherance is hardly unique to our own age, with its "Prince" Mike Romanoff or the Calypso "Lord" Invader.

In the early eighteenth century, we find a "Lord" Timothy Dexter, of Newburyport, Massachusetts, where, it is said, he "lived in vulgar magnificence," in a splendid mansion on a fine estate. Here is his story as reported late in the century:

Timothy Dexter was born in 1743, in Malden, Massachusetts. Apprenticed by his father to a leather dresser at the age of 21 he embarked in a business of his own and carried it on successfully. He amassed a large sum of money by buying depreciated notes and selling them for their full nominal value, and by marrying a rich widow. Having secured a liberal fortune, he set himself up as "Lord Timothy Dexter" in a Newburyport mansion. Everything about him was unique and absurd. Fifteen thousand dollars worth of wooden statues adorned his grounds. His dress was a mixture of a Captain of militia and a Roman senator; and his literary composures were as odd and stupid as he was himself. His *Pickle for the Knowing Ones, or Plain Truth in a Homespun Dress* is a collection of proverbs, aphorisms and observations, new and old, so wretchedly written that it is difficult to discover their meaning. The second edition of this book bore this note on the last page: 'Fourder mister printer the Nowing ones complane of my book the fust edition had no stops I put in a nuf here and they may pepper and solt it as they please'.

"I heartily disapprove," said Dr. Sam. "A man must be able to live with his own handle as if it were his ears. To seek to gain a grander monicker is to make a silk ear out of a sow's purse!" And on further reflection he added, "Your father gave you the name of Burl Icle Ivanhoe because he believed in my philosophy, that to be a man requires that you accept everything life has to give you beginning with your name."

AMERICA'S UNCLAIMED UNACCLAIMED
NATIONAL ANTHEM

Looking at the patriotic songs associated with the history of the United States, one discovers a surprising thing. There is one song that has accompanied almost all the historical events of this country; it is the most persistently sung and yet the most persistently ignored song in American history. It is the song every schoolboy knows and yet it is the least respected of songs. It is America's unacclaimed national anthem—"Yankee Doodle."

In the Colonies, the first appearance of this melody was 1755, during the French and Indian War. Braddock was in Albany organizing an expedition against Niagara and Frontenac. Two bodies of troops were assembling, the English regulars and the colonials. Compared to the British the colonials were a ragged and badly organized group. Dr. Shuckburg, one of the English Army surgeons, made fun of the motley colonials by referring to them as "Yankee Doodles" in a satirical poem. He put his poem to the melody of an English country dance. One of the colonial band leaders asked what was the latest English marching song and was given this dance melody as a joke. Not knowing about the words, the colonials marched to the melody while the English troops laughed to see the ill-dressed colonials marching to a tune for which there were words making fun of these same colonials.

Unfortunately, Dr. Shuckburg's words are lost. But sometime

before the Revolutionary War, a colonial wit summarized the history of the Colonies to date and put it to this tune. As you will see it is a most prideful account of the bravery of the early settlers. The term, "Yankee Doodle," is used with conscious pride:

If, Yankees, you would have a song,
A deucèd nation fine one;
Then in the chorus all along,
I guess you'd like to join one.

Our grandsires lived a long way off,
And if you think to doubt it;
And I had only time enough,
I'd tell you all about it.

I'd tell you all, how hard they were,
For tithes and taxes hinted;
And how they didn't think 'twas fair,
And how they got affronted.

And now of what might them befall,
They nothing were afraid in;
So took their wives and children all,
And off they push'd for Leyden.

And there they got a monstrous ship,
As big as any gunboat;
And all to fit her for a trip,
I guess was nicely done to 't.

Then Yankee Doodle all aboard!
Pip'd out the boatswain handy;
And young and old struck up and roar'd,
Yankee Doodle Dandy.

Then ev'r man, he seiz'd a rope,
And pull'd with all his soul, Sir;
And haul'd the tow-cloth all way up,
And ti'd it to the pole, Sir.

Then Yankee Doodle now they go,
All in their ship so handy;
And sing All-Saints, Old Hundred, too,
And Yankee Doodle Dandy.

But when they got away from shore,
And 'fore the wind did streak it;
And heard the ocean billows roar,
I guess they didn't like it.

But Yankee Doodle, never mind,
Strike up the chorus handy;
They'd left the oppressors far behind,
So Yankee Doodle Dandy.

The billows they roll'd up on high,
Enough the ship to fill, Sir;
And toss'd the vessel at the sky,
As high as 'chusett Hill, Sir.

But foul or fair, we're stout and strong,
In ev'ry lot we're handy;
Then join the chorus, and the song,
Of Yankee Doodle Dandy.

And there they saw a great big fish,
That thrash'd about his tail, Sir;
And look so deuced saucyish,
I guess it was a whale, Sir.

And now this noble ship, once more
As staunch as ever man trod;
Approach'd the sandy, desert shore,
And landed them on Cape Cod.

When all were safely landed so,
Our grand-daddies and grand-dams;
And Sall, and Sue, and Bill, and Joe,
All had a feast on Sand-clams!

To keep the bears and panthers out,
And not less savage wild-man;
Of white pine logs each built a hut,
As big as father's hog-pen.

They planted fields enclos'd with stakes,
And work'd like dogs or asses;
Made pumpkin pies and Indian cakes,
And ate them up with 'lasses.

And ev'ry day for many weeks,
Beginning on each Monday;
They watch'd and work'd and fought like Greeks
And went to church on Sunday.

This was only the beginning. Every war and every political campaign in American history has had its verses to the "Yankee Doodle" melody from then to now, for the melody is an excellent complement to short, terse statements.

26

SOME STORIES CURRENT
IN THE COLONIES

We forget in these settled days that living with the Indians or maintaining themselves against the Indians was a basic problem to the early settlers. Yet these settlers made their own difficulties through bad treatment of the Indians. The settlers often recognized the resentment of the Indians as natural. Here are three stories from colonial days:

1. *Deception:* The captain of a vessel, having a desire to make a present to a lady of some fine oranges which he had just brought from "the sugar islands," gave them to an Indian in his employ to carry to her. Lest he should not perform the office punctually, he wrote a letter to her, to be taken along with the present, that she might detect the bearer, if he should fail to deliver the whole of what he was entrusted with. The Indian, during the journey, reflected how he should refresh himself with the oranges, and not be found out. Not having any apprehension of the manner of communication by writing, he concluded that it was only necessary to keep his design secret from the letter itself, supposing that it would tell on him if he did not; he therefore laid it upon the ground, and rolled a large stone upon it, and retired to some distance, where he regaled himself with several oranges, and then proceeded on his journey.

On delivering the remainder and the letter to the lady, she asked him where the rest of the oranges were; he said he had delivered all; she told him that the letter said there were several more sent; to which he answered that the letter lied, and she must not believe it. But he was soon confronted in his falsehood, and, begging forgiveness of the offense, was pardoned.

2. *Matrimony:* An aged Indian, who for many years had spent much time among the white people, both in Pennsylvania and New Jersey, one day, about the year 1770, observed that the Indians had not only a much easier way of getting a wife than the whites, but also a more certain way of getting a good one. For, said he in broken English, "white men court—court—maybe one whole year! maybe two years before he marry! Well—maybe then he get good wife—but maybe not—may be very cross! Well, now suppose cross! scold so soon as get awake in the morning! scold all day! scold until sleep! all one—he must keep him! White people have law forbidding throw away wife he be ever so cross—must keep him always! Well, how Indian do? Indian, when he see industrious squaw, he go to him, place his two forefingers close aside each other, make two like one—then look squaw in the face—see him smile—this is all one he say yes! so he take him home—no danger he be cross! No, no—squaw know too well what Indian do if he cross! throw him away and take another! Squaw love to eat meat—no husband, no meat. Squaw do everything to please husband, he do everything to please squaw—live happy."

3. *Justice:* A white trader sold a quantity of powder to an Indian, and imposed upon him by making him believe it was a grain that grew like wheat, by sowing it upon the ground. He was greatly elated by the prospect, not only of raising his own powder, but of being able to supply others, and thereby becoming immensely rich. Having prepared

his ground with great care, he sowed his powder with the utmost exactness in the spring. Month after month passed away, but his powder did not even sprout, and winter came before he was satisfied that he had been deceived. He said nothing; but some time after, when the trader had forgotten the trick, the same Indian succeeded in getting credit of him to a large amount. The time set for paying having expired, the trader sought out the Indian at his residence, and demanded payment for his goods. The Indian heard his demand with great complaisance; then looking him shrewdly in the eye, said, "Me pay you when my powder grow." This was enough. The guilty white man quickly retraced his steps, satisfied, we apprehend, to balance his account with the chagrin he had received.

Which puts me in mind of what Dr. Sam said to my father when he returned home from a trip to find the whisky, which he had hidden away in the barn for some special occasion, had been stolen. On complaining of this to Dr. Sam, he got the all-too-true answer, "Why, Frank, honest people will steal whisky."

DR. FRANKLIN'S MORAL CODE

Our great American philosopher and statesman, Benjamin Franklin, drew up the following list of moral virtues, to which he paid constant and earnest attention, and, he said, "thereby made myself a better and happier man."

TEMPERANCE. Eat not to fullness; drink not to elevation.

SILENCE. Speak not but what may benefit others or yourself; avoid trifling conversation.

ORDER. Let all your things have their places; let each part of your business have its time.

RESOLUTION. Resolve to perform what you ought; perform without fail what you resolve.

FRUGALITY. Make no expense, but do good to others as yourself; that is, waste nothing.

INDUSTRY. Lose no time, be always employed in something useful; but avoid all unnecessary actions.

SINCERITY. Use no hurtful deceit; think innocently and justly; and, if you speak, speak accordingly.

JUSTICE. Wrong no one by doing injuries, or omitting the benefits that are your duty.

MODERATION. Avoid extremes; forbear resenting injuries.

CLEANLINESS. Suffer no uncleanliness in body, clothes, or habitation.

TRANQUILITY. Be not disturbed about trifles, or at accidents common or unavoidable.

HUMILITY. Imitate Jesus Christ.

THE FASHION FOR MEN

Men's fashions in America in the late eighteenth century fell into two categories: the dress of the frontier and the polished dress of the city. In the city itself there were two classes of dress—that used by officials and men of wealth and the dress of the average man. We find from an old *Colony Memorial* this description of how men dressed in the more civilized communities:

In general, men old and young, who had got their growth, had a decent coat, vest and small clothes, [breeches] and some kind of fur hat. These were for holiday use and would last half a lifetime. Old men had a great coat and a pair of boots. The boots generally lasted for life. For common use they had a long jacket, or what was called a fly coat, reaching down about halfway to the knee. They had a striped jacket to wear made of flannel cloth.

They had flannel shirts and stockings and thick leather shoes. A silk handkerchief for holidays would last ten years. In summertime they had a pair of wide trousers reaching halfway from the knee to the ankle.

Shoes and stockings were not worn by the young men. Few men in farming wore them either. As for boys, as soon as they were taken out of petticoat, they were put into small clothes summer and winter. This lasted till they put on long trousers which they called tongs, made of linen or cotton. 'Young men never thought of great coats and overcoats were then unknown.'

As long as clothes were made in the home, this kind of wardrobe no doubt sufficed. But when the thread began to be spun outside, the cloth to be woven in a textile factory, the goods cut in a men's wear industry and the finished product marketed in stores that found it necessary to advertise their wares, the mere necessity of decent clothes gave way to the competitive pleasure of owning them.

On the frontier, the hunters, scouts and frontiersmen wore clothes that were partly from the East and partly bought from the Indians. They would barter the Indians liquor, beads or anything at hand in exchange for pieces of Indian dress. In his notes on the Indian Wars, Joseph Doddridge has this to say:

The hunting shirt was universally worn. This was a kind of loose frock, reaching halfway down the thighs, with large sleeves, open before, and so wide as to lap over a foot or more when belted. The cape was large, and sometimes handsomely fringed with a raveled piece of cloth of a different color from that of the hunting shirt itself. The bosom of this dress served as a wallet to hold a chunk of bread, cakes, jerk, tow for wiping the barrel of the rifle, or any other necessary for the hunter or warrior. The belt, which was always tied behind, answered several purposes, besides that of holding the dress together. In cold weather, the mittens, and sometimes the bullet-bag, occupied the front part of it. To the right side was suspended the tomahawk and to the left the scalping knife in its leathern sheath. The hunting shirt was generally made of linsey, sometimes of coarse linen, and a few of dressed deer skins. These last were very cold and uncomfortable in wet weather. The shirt and jacket were of the common fashion.

In the later years of the Indian War our young men became more enamored of the Indian dress throughout, with the exception of the matchcoat. The drawers were laid aside and the leggins made longer, so as to reach the upper part of the thigh. The Indian breech clout was adopted. This was a piece of linen or cloth nearly a yard long, and eight or nine inches broad. This passed under the belt before and behind leaving the ends for flaps hanging before and behind over the belt. These flaps were sometimes ornamented with some coarse kind of embroidery work. To the same belts which secured the breech clout, strings which supported the long leggins were attached. When this belt, as was often the case, passed over the hunting shirt the upper part of the thighs and part of the hips were naked.

The young warrior instead of being abashed by this nudity was proud of his Indian-like dress. In some few instances I have seen them go into places of public worship in this dress. Their appearance, however, did not add much to the devotion of the young ladies.

AMERICA'S UNCLAIMED UNACCLAIMED NATIONAL ANTHEM YANKEE DOODLE: THE AMERICAN REVOLUTION

In the period leading up to the Revolutionary War, feeling ran high. Once again British soldiers sang "Yankee Doodle" verses derogatorily. Outside of the churches they annoyed Bostonians by singing:

> Yankee Doodle came to town,
> For to buy a firelock;
> We will tar and feather him
> And so we will John Hancock.

The basic melody was English, and the British troops marched from Boston to Lexington to its tune. At this point the colonials called the song "The Lexington March."

However, ignoring English verses, the colonials proudly sang a "Yankee Doodle" song about General Washington and the Continental Army that put the British in Boston to rout. These are the verses we all know. The allusions in this song to Washington, his "slapping stallion," and the motley army, are very interesting as showing how the Continental Army looked to itself.

Father and I went down to camp,
Along with Captain Good'n
And there we saw the men and boys
As thick as hasty puddin'.

(Chorus)
> Yankee Doodle keep it up,
> Yankee Doodle Dandy,
> Mind the music and the step
> And with the girls be handy.

There was Captain Washington
Upon a slapping stallion,
Giving orders to his men—
I guess there was a million.

And then the feathers on his hat,
They look'd so tarnal fina,
I wanted peskily to get
To give to my Jemina.

And there they had a swampin' gun
As large as log of maple,
On a deuced little cart—
A load for Father's cattle.

And every time they fired it off,
It took a horn of powder;
It made a noise like Father's gun,
Only a nation louder.

And Captain Davis had a gun,
He kind-a clapt his hand on't
And stuck a crooked stabbing iron
Upon the little end on't.

And there I see a pumpkin shell,
As big as Mother's basin,
And every time they touch'd it off,
They scamper'd like the nation.

And there I see a little keg,
Its heads were made of leather—
They knock'd upon't with little sticks
To call the folks together.

There they fife away like fun,
And play on cornstock fiddles,
And some had ribands red as blood,
All wound about their middles.

The troopers, too, would gallop up
And fire right in our faces;
It scar'd me almost half to death
To see them run such races.

I see another snarl of men
A-digging graves, they told me,
So tarnal long, so tarnal deep,
They tended they should hold me.

But I can't tell you half I see
They kept up such a smother;
So I took my hat off—made a bow,
And scamper'd home to Mother.

There is a tendency to speak of the Continental soldier as ill-prepared and untrained. Actually, the Continental Army was unorganized as to army discipline, but its soldiers were excellent marksmen. They had had practical training in the use of arms by the necessity of continual preparation against the Indians and French. At least one-fifth of all able-bodied men in the

Colonies had probably fought in the field during the French and Indian War. Moreover, under the instruction of the Provincial Congress of 1775, every village green had been drilling, particularly in Massachusetts.

Washington himself, although his ability as a soldier has been questioned, fought courageously through the French and Indian War and had trained in the Virginia militia. As Thomas Jefferson pointed out, Washington was the greatest horseman of his time. He was also rightfully proud of his own horses and when he left Virginia to assume command of the Continental Army (then besieging the British in Boston) he brought with him five horses of his own breeding. One of these is probably the "slapping stallion" of the verse.

One recalls from the history books that the original strategy of the British in the American Revolutionary War was to divide the Colonies into three parts: General Burgoyne was to march down from Canada through Lake Champlain to Albany; General Howe was to come up to Albany from New York; General St. Leger was to join them from the Mohawk Valley. There are "Yankee Doodle" comments on all the campaigns and on several of the battles, and on various incidents.

For example, General Burgoyne was most unpopular. His amours were celebrated, his unlikable traits well known and he was an ideal subject for a ballad. He was defeated at Saratoga and the Colonies sang to the tune of "Yankee Doodle":

> When Jack the King's commander,
> Was going to his duty;
> Through all the crowd he smiled and bow'd
> To every blooming beauty.

> The city run with feats he'd done,
> In Portugal and Flanders;
> And all the town thought he'd be crown'd,
> The first of Alexanders.

To Hampton Court he first repairs,
To kiss great George's hand, Sirs;
Then to harangue on state affairs,
Before he left the land, Sirs.

The "Lower House" sat mute as mouse,
To hear his grand orations
And "all the peers," with loudest cheers,
Proclaimed him to the nation.

Then off he went to Canada,
Next to Ticonderoga;
And quitting those away he goes,
Straightway to Saratoga.

With great parade his march he made,
To gain his wished-for station;
While far and wide his minions fled,
To spread his "proclamation."

To such as stayed he offers made,
Of "pardon on submission;
But savage bands should ease the lands,
Of all in opposition."

But ah, the cruèl fates of war!
This boasted son of Britain;
When mounting his triumphal car,
With sudden fear was smitten.

The Sons of Freedom gathered 'round,
His hostile bands confounded;
And when they'd fain have turned their back,
They found themselves surrounded.

The British Fleet was in the Delaware River. An American,
Mr. Bushnell, had an ingenious idea. He decided that he would

float kegs loaded with gunpowder down the river and that these would explode on contact with the British ships. Once aware of this, the British were panic-stricken and fired at every object floating in the river. While they were doing this, General Howe was summoned forth in all haste.

Francis Hopkinson, one of the first American composers, a good friend of General Washington, and a signer of the Declaration of Independence, was extremely amused both by the incident and by the gossip that General William Howe lay snoring in bed during the initial part of this incident . . . and not alone. With him was the wife of a Tory whom Howe had made Commissioner of Prisoners. To the tune of "Yankee Doodle" Hopkinson made up a ballad entitled "The Battle of the Kegs." His version of this battle immediately became popular with all the Continental officers and army:

> Gallants attend and hear a friend
> Trill forth harmonious ditty,
> Strange things I'll tell which late befell
> In Philadelphia city.

> 'Twas early day, as poets say,
> Just when the sun was rising,
> A soldier stood on a log of wood,
> And saw a thing surprising.

> As in amaze he stood to gaze,
> The truth can't be deny'd, sir,
> He spy'd a score of kegs or more
> Come floating down the tide, sir.

> A sailor too in jerkin blue,
> This strange appearance viewing,
> First rubb'd his eye, in great surprise,
> Then said, "Some mischief's brewing.

"These kegs, I'm told, the rebels bold,
Pack'd up like pickling herring;
And they're come down t'attack the town,
In this new way of ferrying."

The soldier flew, the sailor too,
And scar'd almost to death, Sir,
Wore out their shoes, to spread the news,
And ran till out of breath, Sir . . .

Now up and down throughout the town
Most frantic scenes were acted:
Some ran here, and some ran there,
Like men almost distracted.

Some fire cry'd, which some deny'd,
But said the earth had quakèd;
And girls and boys, with hideous noise,
Ran through the street half naked.

Sir William he, snug as a flea,
Lay all this time a-snoring,
Nor dream'd of harm as he lay warm,
In bed with Mrs. Loring.

Now in a fright, he starts upright,
Awak'd by such a clatter;
He rubs both eyes, and boldly cries,
"For God's sake, what's the matter?"

At his bedside he then espy'd
Sir Erskine at command, Sir,
Upon one foot, he had one boot,
And th'other in his hand, Sir.

"Arise, arise," Sir Erskine cries,
"The rebels—more's the pity.

Without a boat, are all afloat
And rang'd before the city."

"The motley crew, in vessels new,
With Satan for their guide, Sir;
Pack'd up in bags, or wooden kegs,
Come driving down the tide, Sir.

"Therefore prepare for bloody war,
These kegs must all be routed,
Or surely we'll despisèd be,
And British courage doubted."

The royal band, now ready stand
All rang'd in dread array, Sir;
With stomach stout to see it out,
And make a bloody day, Sir.

The cannons roar from shore to shore,
The small arms make a rattle;
Since wars began I'm sure no man
E'er saw so strange a battle.

The rebel dales, the rebel vales,
With rebel trees surrounded;
The distant woods, the hills and floods,
With rebel echoes sounded.

The fish below swam to and fro,
Attack'd from every quarter;
Why, sure, thought they the mischief's to pay
'Mongst folks above the water.

The kegs, 'tis said, though strongly made,
Of rebel staves and hoops, Sir;

Could not oppose their pow'rful foes,
The conqu'ring British troops, Sir.

From morn to night these men of might
Display'd amazing courage;
And when the sun was fairly down
Return'd to sup their porridge.

An hundred men with each a pen,
Or more, upon my word, Sir,
It is most true, would be too few,
Their valor to record, Sir.

Such feats they did perform that day,
Against those wicked kegs, Sir.
That years to come, if they get home,
They'll make their boasts and brags, Sir.

General Cornwallis, the most effective British general in America, won Charleston and Savannah. Because of this the American, General Gates, was replaced by General Greene. He and Cornwallis fought back and forth over the North Carolina-South Carolina boundary. A wit of the time called this back-and-forth movement "Cornwallis' Country Dance." The ballad describing this seems to have been sung to both a variant of "Pop Goes the Weasel" and "Yankee Doodle." Here is "Cornwallis' Country Dance" to the tune of "Yankee Doodle":

Cornwallis led a country dance,
The like was never seen, Sir;
Much retrograde and much advance,
And all with General Greene, Sir.
They rambled up, they rambled down,
Joined hands and off they run, Sir;
General Greene to Charles Town,
The Earl to Wilmington, Sir.

Quoth he, my guards are weary grown,
With doing country dances;
They never at St. James had shown,
At capers, kicks, or prances.
No men so gallant there were seen,
While saunt'ring on parade, Sir;
Or dancing o'er the park so green,
Or at the masquerade, Sir.

Good Washington, Columbia's son,
Whom easy nature taught, Sir;
Has grace which can't by pains be won,
Or Pluto's gold be bought, Sir.
Now hand in hand they circle round,
In every dancing mood, Sir;
The gentle movement soon confounds,
The Earl's day draws near, Sir.

His music soon forgets to play,
His feet can't move no more, Sir;
And all his men now curse the day,
They jiggèd to our shore, Sir.
Now Tories all, what can you say . . .
Cornwallis is no griper;
But while your hopes are danced away,
It's you that pay the piper.

After Cornwallis surrendered, there was an important debate
about what music was to be played for the surrender ceremonies. Each side had to play its own song. Strangely and fittingly,
the British played a current popular song from England, "The
World Turned Upside Down." The American Army played its
most famous song with great pride—"Yankee Doodle."

AMERICA'S FIRST NAVAL HERO

Any organized effort of human beings needs a symbol. Usually it is necessary to invent one. Fortunately, sometimes a living symbol emerges so vital and inspiring as to remain a symbol from generation to generation. Such was John Paul Jones to the American Navy and all of us who love the sea. John Paul Jones could sail a ship and he could maneuver her to his will. He was a true sailor.

There were eighteen naval officers in the Navy of the American Revolutionary Forces but only one, John Paul Jones, is well known. "The North Carolina Captain" emerged as a great fighting sailor. There were others who continued the Navy tradition through the war with the Barbary pirates, but Jones is the only hero of this early war.

He was born John Paul in Scotland. As a boy he was apprenticed to the Royal Navy. He early left the Navy and went into the slave trade. We hear of him as third mate of the brig *The King George* and chief mate of the *Two Friends*. The crew of the latter boat mutinied and for a time John Paul was sought by the authorities for killing the ringleader. During the period when he was hiding out, there is evidence that he lived as a pirate in the West Indies, which at that time was the home of outlaws of all kinds from all parts of the world.

Paul became quite excited by the revolutionary cause and turned up in North Carolina. Here he found a patron in Joseph

Hughes, an influential shipowner. When out of necessity the Continental Congress had to commission privateers to fight their naval battles, Hughes requested a commission for John Paul Jones.

Before John Paul Jones went into active service under the Continental Congress, Washington wrote a letter of recommendation to the Maritime Committee of the Congress in which he outlined certain necessary qualifications for the new navy. Washington commented: "Mr. Jones is clearly not only a master mariner within the scope of the art of navigation, but he also holds a strong and profound sense of the political and military way of men of the sea. His powers of usefulness are great and must be constantly kept in view."

Jones's most famous fighting was done off the coast of England. His first ship was the *Ranger*. We learn from a contemporary that his crew grumbled mightily because there was only one barrel of rum aboard when the *Ranger* sailed for European waters. Jones, as was usual for him, drove his men to the full capacity of their powers, and the lack of rum did not help their tempers. However, Lieutenant Hall, who kept a record of his voyage with Jones, wrote:

I had sailed with many captains, in all kinds of voyages, but I had never seen a ship crowded as Captain Jones drove the *Ranger*. . . . Imagine, then, the situation of the *Ranger's* crew, with a top-heavy and crank ship under their feet, and a commander who day and night insisted on every rag she could stagger under without laying clear down.

As it was, she came close to beam-ends more than once, and on one occasion righted only by letting fly sheets out with hatchets. During all this trying work, Captain Jones was his own navigating officer, keeping the deck eighteen or twenty hours out of every twenty-four.

One of Jones' most famous fights was when his ship *Bon Homme Richard* fought the English ship *Serapis* and won. In his ship's log, Jones describes the formal surrender of the commander of the *Serapis*:

Captain Pearson now confronted me, the image of chagrin and despair. He offered me his sword with a slight bow, but was silent. His first lieutenant followed suit. I was sorry for them, for they had fought their ship better and braver than any English ship was ever fought before, and this fortune of war came hard to them. I wanted to speak, but they were so sad and dignified in their silence, I hardly knew what to say. Finally, I mustered courage and said, as I took the swords and handed them to Midshipman Potter at my elbow, "Captain Pearson, you have fought heroically. You have worn this sword to your own credit and to the honor of your service. I hope your sovereign will suitably reward you." He bowed again, but made no reply, whereupon I requested him and his lieutenant to accompany Mr. Potter to my cabin.

The *Bon Homme Richard* herself sank, toward evening of the day after the victory over the *Serapis*. After the wounded American officers had been transferred, with the crew and the English prisoners, Paul Jones left the *Richard* last of all, and watched his ship go down. In his journal, Jones wrote:

The ensign-gaff, shot away in action, had been fished and put in place soon after firing ceased, and our torn and tattered flag was left flying when we abandoned her. As she plunged down by the head at the last, her taffrail momentarily rose in the air; so the very last vestige mortal eyes ever saw of the *Bon Homme Richard* was the defiant wavering of her unconquered and unstricken flag as she went down. And as I had given them the good old ship for their sepulchre, I now bequeathed to my immortal dead the flag they had so desperately defended for their winding-sheet!

And soon America was singing a ballad that has lived to this day:

> 'Tis of a gallant Yankee ship
>   that flew the stripes and stars,
> And the whistling wind from the west nor'west
>   blew through the pitch-pine spars,
> With her starboard tacks aboard, my boys,
>   she hung upon the gale;
> On an autumn night we raised the light
>   on the old head of Kinsale.
>
> It was a clear and cloudless night,
>   and the wind blew steady and strong,
> As fairly over the sparkling deep
>   our good ship bowled along;
> With the foaming seas beneath her bow
>   the fiery waves she spread
> And sending low her bosom of snow,
>   she buried her lee, cathead.
>
> There was no talk of short'ning sail
>   by him who walked the poop,
> And under the press of her pond'ring jib
>   the boom bent like a hoop!
> And the groaning waterways told the strain
>   that held her stout main tack,
> But he only laughed as he glanced aloft
>   at a white and silv'ry track.
>
> The nightly robes our good ship wore
>   were her own topsails three,
> Her spanker and her standing jib,
>   the courses being free;
> Now lay aloft! my heroes bold,
>   let not a moment pass!

And royals and topgallant sails
  were quickly on each mast.

What looms upon our starboard bow?
  What hangs upon the breeze?
'Tis time our good ship hauled her wind
  abreast the old saltee's.
For by her ponderous press of sail
  and by her escorts four,
We saw our morning visitor
  was a British man-of-war.

Up spoke our noble captain then,
  and a shot ahead of us passed,
"Haul snug your flowing courses!
  Lay your topsail to the mast!"
Those Englishmen gave three loud hurrahs
  from the deck of their covered ark
And we answered back by a solid broadside
  from the deck of our patriot bark.

"Out booms! Out booms!" our skipper cried,
  "Out booms and give her sheet,"
And the swiftest keel that ever was launched
  shot ahead of the British fleet,
And amidst a thundering shower of shot
  with the stun-sails hoisting away,
Down the north channel Paul Jones did steer
  just at the break of day.

  The report of the exploits of Jones and the other privateers
gave the rebelling colonists belief in their Navy. By the end of
1776 there were at sea 136 privateers with commissions from the
Naval Committee of the Continental Congress. And, as the War
progressed, the privateers grew in size.
  Elias Derby of Salem, a wealthy shipowner, began to study

and execute new designs, rigging and armament of schooner privateers that could successfully fight the British sloops of war. He and other shipowners began to build boats that could mount more than twenty guns, could be manned by at least 150 men, were fast enough to run away from more heavily-gunned ships and could be converted to cargo-carrying vessels.

It is an interesting point that in order to get reluctant seamen to sign articles and come aboard, the owners of vessels kept running tavern bills. It did not matter whether men were brought aboard drunk or sober. One of Mr. Derby's tavern bills was £1500 for one month, for 113 bowls of punch, grog and cherry toddy. The names of these early privateers are as dramatic as the life led aboard them: *Wildcat and Liberty, Black Snake, Revenge, Blood Hound,* etc.

THE FAMILY TREE

Doctor Sam was a traveling medicine man, an uncle to me as he was to half of the United States, a doctor for ills of the spirit as well as of the body, for which he carried poems, pills, and panaceas of his own makings.

He was never averse to telling you the history of his fore-bears. He was particularly fond of his great-grandfather, Brother Jonathan, who was the young immigrant brother—underfed and ill-clad—of the paunchy, splendidly waistcoated John Bull of English fame. Brother Jonathan came to America penniless in the early 1800's and after a year in Boston found that he had a light heart and a wayward foot and spent his life traveling up and down the eastern states, a wanderer given to swapping.

Brother Jonathan helped to populate the American continent. We are told he had a daughter in Charleston, a son in New York, and another in Cambridge, Massachusetts. His Cambridge scion, Sam Jonathan, did not attend Harvard, but by proximity to that august seat of learning, he did acquire a professorial desire to lecture. He traveled the United States as an actor given to monologues and lectures revealing the humorous aspects of the astringent Yankee character. This amused the Yankees who liked to laugh at themselves, but England and Europe called Sam "Uncle" and turned the jokes to make him and his countrymen look foolish. The twist did not succeed, for the fun-loving Americans enjoyed the shafts as jokes and would not take the barbs to heart.

The New York son, Jack Downing, after his mother, was the youngest of Brother Jonathan's get. He inherited his father's aptitude for swapping, but finding words a more profitable swap, especially in Washington where words were legal tender and humor at a premium, he appointed himself advisor to "The Old Gineral" as he called President Jackson.

Meantime, his father, Brother Jonathan, was ailing, for the European barbs that had attacked him as "awkward, ungainly, illiterate and uncouth" had stabbed him to the heart. He was forsaken by his wealthier friends who immediately sent their sons to school abroad to avoid his influence.

"A clown's cap can make anyone look like a fool, remember that," Dr. Sam explained one day when he and I were putting flowers on Brother Jonathan's grave. "He took it too much to heart. If the cap fits, wear it, they say. Well, make sure you choose the right kind of cap." Dr. Sam set his own headpiece fair and square again on his forehead. "If you pay as much heed to other men's hats as you do to your own, a cap cannot ever make a fool of you."

In Carolina, Brother Jonathan's daughter, Abigail, married a Hezekiah Bigelow, a New England shipowner. Their issue was uneventful, but a nephew of Hezekiah, much influenced by Abigail's tales of her brother, Sam Jonathan, "Lecturier Extraordinaire," took off across the country westward. He made the journey twenty times and even participated in the California gold rush, during which fortune did not bestow the favor of any gold, but he did become famous the land over as Sam Slick, the peddler. It is this same Sam Slick who was the natural father of Dr. Samuel Icle Ivanhoe, my great good friend; and it was from Sam Slick that Dr. Sam learned to talk in rhyme and philosophical generalities instead of the Yankee prose rhythms that were the natural tongue of his forebears.

While Sam Slick was making his second journey across America, his hero, Sam Jonathan, died. Upon his death he received obituaries from all over this world that identified him with his sire, Brother Jonathan, who had died unnoticed. It was a matter of pride to the family and to Sam Slick, who regarded himself as one of them, that there was affection tinging the contempt with which the world called him America's "Uncle Sam" and made him the symbol of the growing country.

32

AN ENGLISHMAN IN DEFENSE OF
COLONIAL ENGLISHMEN: 1773

Many English statesmen sided with the colonial resistance to
taxation without representation, especially taxation for the eco-
nomic benefit of those whose interests were far from colonial
interests. William Pitt, later Earl of Chatham, not only opposed
the Stamp Act of 1766, which was punitive only in purpose and
benefited no one, he said in Parliament that year:

The gentleman tells us America is obstinate; America is
almost in open rebellion. I rejoice that America has re-
sisted. Three millions of people so dead to all the feelings
of liberty, as voluntarily to submit to be slaves, would have
been fit instruments to make slaves of the rest. A great
deal has been said without doors of the power, of the
strength of America. It is a topic that ought to be cau-
tiously meddled with. In a good cause, on a sound bottom,
the force of this country can crush America to atoms. I
know the valour of your troops. I know the skill of your
officers. . . . But on this ground, on the Stamp Act, when
so many here will think it is a crying injustice, I am one
who will lift up my hand against it.

The Americans have not acted in all things with prudence and temper. The Americans have been wronged.
They have been driven to madness by injustice. Will you

punish them for the madness you have occasioned? Rather let prudence and temper come first from this side. I will undertake for America, that she will follow the example. . . .

Upon the whole, I will beg leave to tell the House what is really my opinion. It is, that the Stamp Act be repealed absolutely, totally, and immediately.

THE AMERICAN VICAR OF BRAY

The original Vicar of Bray was an English clergyman who managed to reconcile himself to changing religious positions without a qualm of conscience. He four times changed from Papist to Protestant and back again. Taxed with being a "turncoat," the Vicar said, "Not so, neither; for if I changed my religion, I am sure I kept true to my principle, which is, to live and to die the Vicar of Bray."

And so he did, for no matter who was king, this gentleman remained the Vicar of Bray.

During the American Revolution, there were many of the same color—they were Whigs when the colonials came in and Tories when the British were in town. American satirists, like Freneau, whose writings related primarily to public characters and events, had quite a bit to say about the "American Vicar of Bray." His chorus was from the original English broadside but the words applied to the American Revolution:

When Royal George ruled o'er this land,
And loyalty no harm meant,
For church and king I made a stand,
And so I got preferment.

    And this is the law I will maintain
    Until my dying day, sir,
    Let whatsoever king will reign,
    I'll be a Vicar of Bray, sir.

When Stamp Act passed the Parliament,
To bring some grist to mill, sir,
To back it was my firm intent,
But soon there came repeal, sir.

I quickly joined the common cry,
That we should all be slaves, sir,
The House of Commons was a sty,
The King and Lords were knaves, sir.

I laugh'd at all the vain pretense,
Of taxing at this distance,
And swore before I'd pay my pence,
I'd make a firm resistance.

A congress now was quickly call'd,
That we might act together;
I thought that Britain would appalled,
Be glad to make fair weather.

But Britain was not quickly scared,
She told another story;
When Independence was declared,
I figur'd as a Tory.

Declared it was rebellion base,
To take up arms—I cursed it—
For, faith, it seemed a settled case,
That we should soon be worsted.

When penal laws were passed by vote,
I thought The Test a grievance,
Yet sooner than I'd lose a goat,
I swore the States allegiance.

The thin disguise could hardly pass,
For I was much suspected;
I felt myself much like an ass
In lion's skin detected.

And so it went. The best known colonials in the Vicar of Bray category were two newspaper editors: one James Rivington of the *New York Gazette*; the other, Benjamin Towne, editor of *The Pennsylvania Evening Post*. Mr. Rivington had always been a Tory. The paper of which he was editor and proprietor was known as *Rivington's New York Gazetteer* or *The Connecticut Inquirer and Quebec Weekly Advertiser*.

This paper was established in 1773 and was avowedly Tory in its devotion to King George. It was in 1775 that armed men from Connecticut entered Rivington's press in the city, threw the type into heaps and destroyed the presses. Rivington immediately took a boat for London. Here he applied for a grant and received a commission as King's printer for the colonies in America. He was supplied with type and presses with which to restore his newspaper. He could not of course return to New York City until the British had possession of it but when General Howe took over that city, Rivington immediately reestablished publication of his paper. This time he called it *Rivington's New York Loyal Gazette*.

His standards were so extremely low that even the Tories called his paper "The Lying Gazette," for it seems that in his zeal for the success of the redcoats he published news items that were more wishful thinking than truth.

At the close of the war, Rivington discarded allegiance to King George and modified the title of his paper to a new title, *Rivington's Gazette and Universal Advertiser*. It received absolutely no support and had to abandon publication. A spurious confession was published in which he declared that he had always been interested in the colonial corps. Freneau immediately published a satire entitled "Rivington's Confessions," the last verse of which went:

"James Rivington, Printer, of late to the king,
But now a republican—under your wing—
Let me stand where he is—don't push him down hill,
And he'll turn a true Blue Skin, or just what you will."

Benjamin Towne of *The Pennsylvania Evening Post* was the more obvious Vicar of Bray. He was a Whig until the British took possession of Philadelphia, at which time he assailed all Tories in his loyalties to the redcoats. When Philadelphia was evacuated, Towne remained and for the second time became an organ for the Whig party.

After the war, he was shunned by many people, and although he paid high writing rates, many writers refused to have anything to do with him. It was reported that one fine day soon after the meeting of Congress, he met one of the city fathers who advised him "make peace with your country."

Towne cried out his innocence and then finally capitulated asking how he could do it. The city father suggested that he write a piece "acknowledging his fault, professing his repentance, and asking forgiveness."

Towne professed himself completely willing to perform this action because he said his heart was in it but he did not have the proper words. As a result, a "ghost writer" was brought in who wrote the required piece under the supervision of Towne and the city father. The piece was published as Towne's genuine composition and made his reputation as a writer. It was entitled *The Humble Confession, Recantation, and Apology of Benjamin Towne.*

The following facts are well known—1st. That I, Benjamin Towne, used to print the *Pennsylvania Evening Post,* under the protection of Congress, and did frequently, and earnestly, solicit sundry members of the said Congress for dissertations and articles of intelligence, professing myself to be a very firm and zealous friend to American liberty.

2nd. That on the English taking possession of Philadelphia, I turned fairly round, and printed my *Evening Post* under the protection of General Howe and his army, calling the Congress and all their adherents, Rebels, Rascals, and Raggamuffins, and several other unsavoury names, with which the humane and polite English are pleased to honour them—neither did I ever refuse to insert any dissertation however scurrilous, or any article of intelligence sent to me, altho' many of them I well knew to be, as a certain gentleman elegantly expresses it, facts that never happened.

3rd. That I am now willing and desirous to turn once more, to unsay all that I have last said, and to print and publish for the United States of America, which are likely to be uppermost, against the British Tyrant; nor will I be backward in calling him, after the example of the great and eminent author of Common Sense, *The Royal Brute,* or giving him any other appellation still more opprobrious, if such can be found.

The rational moralists of the last age used to tell us that there was an essential difference between virtue and vice, because there was an essential difference to be observed in the nature and reason of things. Now, with all due deference to these great men, I think I am as much of a Philosopher as to know that there are no circumstances of action more important than those of time and place, therefore, if a man pay no regard to the changes that may happen in these circumstances, there will be very little Virtue, and still less Prudence in his behaviour. Perhaps I have got rather too deep for common readers, and therefore shall ask any plain Quaker in this city, what he would say to a man who should wear the same coat in summer as in winter in

118

this climate? He would certainly say, "Friend, thy wisdom is not great." Now whether I have not had as good reason to change my conduct as my coat, since last January, I leave to every impartial person to determine. 2dly, I do hereby declare and confess, that when I printed for Congress, and on the side of Liberty, it was not by any means from principle, or a desire that the cause of Liberty should prevail, but purely and simply from the love of gain. I could have made nothing but tar and feathers by printing against them as things then stood. I make this candid acknowledgment not only as a penitent to obtain pardon, but to show that there was more consistency in my conduct than my enemies are willing to allow. They are pleased to charge me with hypocrisy in pretending to be a Whig when I was none. This charge is false; I was neither Whig nor Tory, but a Printer. I detest and abhor hypocrisy. I had no more regard for General Howe or General Clinton, or even for Mrs. Loring or any other of the Chaste Nymphs that attended the fete Champetre, alias Mischianza, when I printed in their behalf, than for the Congress on the day of their retreat. It is pretended that I certainly did in my heart incline to the English, because that I printed much bigger lies and in greater number for them than for the Congress. This is a most false and unjust insinuation. It was entirely the fault of the Congress themselves, who thought fit (being but a new potentate upon the earth) to be much more modest, and keep nearer the truth than their adversaries. Had any of them brought me in a lie as big a mountain it should have issued from my press. This gives me an opportunity of showing the folly as well as malignity of those who are actuated by party spirit; many of them have affirmed that I printed monstrous and incredible lies for General Howe. Now pray what harm could incredible lies do? the only hurt, I conceive, that any lie can do, is by obtaining belief, as a truth; but an incredible lie obtains no

119

belief, and therefore at least must be perfectly harmless. What will those cavilers think, if I should turn this argument against them, and say that the most effectual way to disgrace any cause is to publish monstrous and incredible lies in its favour? In this view, I had not only innocence, but some degree of merit to plead. However, take it which way you will, there never was a lie published in Philadelphia that could bear the least comparison with those published by James Rivington, in New York. Upon the whole I hope the public will attribute my conduct, not to disaffection, but to attachment to my own interest and desire of gain in my profession; a principle, if I mistake not, pretty general and pretty powerful in the present day. 3dly. I hope the public will consider that I have been a timorous man, or, if you will, a coward, from my youth, so that I cannot fight—my belly is so big that I cannot run— and I am so great a lover of eating and drinking that I cannot starve. When those three things are considered, I hope they will fully account for my past conduct, and procure me the liberty of going on in the same uniform tenor for the future. No just judgment can be formed of a man's character and conduct unless every circumstance is taken in and fairly attended to; I therefore hope that this justice will be done in my case. I am also verily persuaded that if all those who are cowards as well as myself, but who are better off in other respects, and therefore can and do run whenever danger is near them, would befriend me, I should have no inconsiderable body on my side. Peace be with the Congress and the army. I mean no reflections; but the world is a wide field, and I wish everybody would do as they would be done by. Finally, I do hereby recant, draw back, eat in, and swallow down, every word that I have ever spoken, written, or printed to the prejudice of the United States of America, hoping it will not only satisfy the good people in general, but also all those scatter-brained fellows, who call one another out to shoot pistols in the air, while they tremble so much they cannot hit the mark. In the meantime I will return to labour with assiduity in my lawful calling, and essays and intelligence as before shall be gratefully accepted by the Public's most obedient humble servant,

BENJAMIN TOWNE.

THE FLAG OF THE UNITED STATES

The arms of General George Washington consisted of three stars in the upper portion and three bars running across the escutcheon. It has been said that the flag accepted by the Continental Congress in June, 1777, was derived from Washington's design. Whether or not this is so, the following is a description of the significance of the different parts of the flag of the new Republic, written by a member of the committee that designed it:

The stars of the new flag represent the new constellation of States rising in the West. The idea was taken from the constellation of Lyra, which in the land of Orpheus signifies harmony. The blue in the field was taken from the edges of the Covenanter's banner, in Scotland, significant of the league-covenant of the United Colonies against oppression, incidentally involving the virtues of vigilance, perseverance and justice. The stars were disposed in a circle symbolizing the perpetuity of the Union; the ring, like the serpent of the Egyptians, signifying eternity. The thirteen stripes showed with the stars, the number of the United Colonies, and denoted the subordination of the States to the Union, as well as equally among themselves. The whole was a blending of the various flags of the army and the white ones of the floating batteries. The red color, which in Roman days was the signal of defiance, denoted daring, and the white purity.

Several flags were used by the Colonies before it was decided that the flag of the thirteen United States be thirteen stripes alternately red and white; that the field be thirteen stars, white on blue, representing a new constellation.

At first, a stripe was added as each new state joined the Union, but the flag became too large. Then the number of stripes was reduced to the original thirteen and instead a star was added for each state in the Union. The proportion of the flag is such that properly made it must be one half as broad as long. The first stripe at the top is red, the next white and these alternate so that the last stripe is red. The blue field for the stars is the width and square of the first seven stripes, four red and three white, and so it is to this day.

35

A PROFILE OF GENERAL WASHINGTON
BY THOMAS JEFFERSON

In a letter dated at Monticello, January 2, 1814, and addressed to his friend, Dr. Walter Jones, Thomas Jefferson presented a portrait of George Washington. I have found this most unique and felt that I have as good as met the Father of His Country after reading:

. . . . I think I knew General Washington intimately and thoroughly; and were I called on to delineate his character, it should be in terms like these. His mind was great and powerful, without being of the very first order; his penetration strong, though not so acute as that of a Newton, Bacon, or Locke; and as far as he saw, no judgment was ever sounder. It was slow in operation, being little aided by invention or imagination, but sure in conclusion. Hence the common remark of his officers, of the advantage he derived from councils of war, where hearing all suggestions, he selected whatever was best; and certainly no general ever planned his battles more judiciously. But if deranged during the course of the action, if any member of his plan was dislocated by sudden circumstances, he was slow in readjustment. The consequence was, that he often failed in the field, and rarely against an enemy in station, as at Boston and York. He was incapable of fear, meeting personal dangers with the calmest unconcern. Perhaps the strongest feature in his character was prudence, never acting until every circumstance, every consideration, was maturely weighed; refraining if he saw a doubt, but, when once decided, going through with his purpose, whatever obstacles opposed. His integrity was most pure, his justice the most inflexible I have ever known, no motives of interest or consanguinity, of friendship or hatred, being able to bias his decision. He was, indeed, in every sense of the words, a wise, a good, and a great man. His temper was naturally irritable and high toned; but reflection and resolution had obtained a firm and habitual ascendency over it. If ever, however, it broke its bonds, he was most tremendous in his wrath. In his expenses he was honorable, but exact; liberal in contributions to whatever promised utility; but frowning and unyielding on all visionary projects, and all unworthy calls on his charity. His heart was not warm in its affections; but he exactly calculated every man's value, and gave him a solid esteem proportioned to it. His person, you know, was fine, his stature exactly what one would wish, his deportment easy, erect and noble; the best horseman of his age, and the most graceful figure that could be seen on horseback. Although in the circle of his friends, where he might be unreserved with safety, he took a free share in conversation, his colloquial talents were not above mediocrity, possessing neither copiousness of ideas, nor fluency of words. In public, when called on for a sudden opinion, he was unready, short and embarrassed. Yet he wrote readily, rather diffusely, in an easy and correct style. This he had acquired by conversation with the world, for his education was merely reading, writing, and common arithmetic, to which he added surveying at a later date. His time was employed in action chiefly, reading little, and that only in agriculture and English history. His correspondence became necessarily extensive, and, with journalizing his agricultural proceedings, occupied most of his leisure hours within doors. On the whole, his character was, in its mass, perfect, in nothing bad, in few points indifferent; and it may truly be said, that never did nature and fortune combine more perfectly to make a man great, and to place him in the same constellation with whatever worthies have merited from a man an everlasting remembrance. For his was the singular destiny and merit, of leading the armies of his country successfully through an arduous war, for the establishment of its independence; of conducting its councils through the birth of a government, new in its forms and principles, until it had settled down into a quiet and orderly train; and of scrupulously obeying the laws through the whole of his career, civil and military, of which the history of the world furnishes no other example.

He has often declared to me that he considered our new Constitution as an experiment on the practicability of republican government, and with what dose of liberty man could be trusted for his own good; that he was determined the experiment should have a fair trial, and would lose the last drop of his blood in support of it. And these declarations he repeated to me the oftener and more pointedly, because he knew my suspicions of Colonel Hamilton's views, and probably had heard from him the same declarations which I had, to wit, "that the British constitution, with its unequal representation, corruption and other existing abuses, was the most perfect government which had ever been established on earth, and that a reformation of those abuses would make it an impracticable government." I do believe that General Washington had not a firm confidence in the durability of our government. He was naturally distrustful of men, and inclined to gloomy apprehensions; and I was ever persuaded that a belief that we must at length end in something like a British constitution had some weight in his adoption of the ceremonies of levees, birthdays, pompous meetings with Congress, and other forms of the same character, calculated to prepare us gradually for a change which he believed possible and let it come on with as little shock as might be to the public mind.

THE STORY OF AN HONORABLE SPY
AND A DISHONORABLE TRAITOR

An English spy who was hanged became a hero to both sides during the American Revolutionary War. This was Major John André of the British Infantry. An American general who was his co-conspirator lived to a ripe old age, anathema to all men. This was General Benedict Arnold of the American armies.

My uncle, Dr. Sam, who had a great reputation as a rhymer, would look at me sternly and recite this acrostic whenever the hated name was mentioned. He claimed to have learned it from his Uncle Sam:

B   orn for a curse to virtue and mankind,
E   arth's broadest realm ne'er knew so black a mind.
N   ight's sable veil your crimes can never hide,
E   ach one so great, 'twould glut historic tide.
D   efunct, your cursed memory will live
I   n all the glare that infamy can give.
C   urses of ages will attend your name,
T   raitors alone will glory in your shame.

A   lmighty vengeance sternly waits to roll
R   ivers of sulphur on your treacherous soul:
N   ature looks shuddering back with conscious dread
O   n such a tarnished blot as she had made.
L   et hell receive you, riveted in chains,
D   oomed to the hottest focus of its flames.

The events that led up to Benedict Arnold's becoming a "traitor" parallel the life story of any young man who continually finds himself maladjusted. Arnold was the grandson of the Colonial Governor of Rhode Island with whom he lived from the early death of his parents. He refused to study and ran away from the Governor at the age of fifteen to take part in an expedition against the French. He deserted the expedition and returned home.

We hear of him again after the battle of Lexington and Concord as a captain in the Massachusetts militia. He enlisted men in an expedition to Fort Ticonderoga. Ethan Allen was ahead of him here and Arnold was forced to serve under him.

When inquiry was made some time later into Benedict Arnold's service under Allen, it was difficult to determine whether psychological antagonism or misjudgment was at fault. In any case Allen was not an easy man to serve under and his reprimands against Arnold were certainly strong. Arnold then went with Montgomery to fight against Canada. With Montgomery he captured Montreal and with Montgomery (who died there) he was defeated at Quebec.

Here, as on many other occasions, Arnold performed many brilliant campaigns. As was often the case, charges of one kind or another were brought against him, and for this reason and because he antagonized everyone, he was never advanced in rank. We find him finally in command of West Point, embittered and moved by a desperate sense of injustice and lack of appreciation.

It was at this time, 1780, that he entered into correspondence with Sir Henry Clinton, the British general, with a view to joining the British forces. He finally planned with Sir Henry to turn West Point over to the British. The man who treatied with him for the British was Major John André. Major André, a personable young Englishman, was caught one night coming out from the American lines. He was challenged by Lt. John

Paulding. Lt. Paulding immediately sent word to Benedict Arnold of his capture of Major André.

Benedict Arnold lost no time in leaving West Point. He joined the British and became a brigadier general; as such, he led an expedition into Virginia and burned Richmond. After that he became Consultant on American Forces to the king and ministry in London. At the end of the American War he was scorned and neglected by the English. Yet he spent the remainder of his life in London fitting out privateers for the West Indies trade. His name became a byword of contempt in both America and England.

II. MAJOR ANDRÉ

The fate of the captive Major André was far more noble. Major André told his story in a letter addressed to General Washington, September 24, 1780, in Salem:

Sir:

What I have as yet said concerning myself was in the justifiable attempt to be extricated; I am too little accustomed to duplicity to have succeeded.

I beg your Excellency will be persuaded that no alteration in the temper of my mind, or apprehension for my safety, induces me to take the step of addressing you, but that it is to rescue myself from an imputation of having assumed a mean character for treacherous purposes or self-interest; a conduct incompatible with the principles that actuate me, as well as with my condition in life.

It is to vindicate my fame that I speak, and not to solicit security.

The person in your possession is Major John André, Adjutant-General to the British army.

The influence of one commander in the army of his adversary is an advantage taken in war. . . .

To favor it, I agreed to meet upon ground not within

the posts of either army, a person who was to give me intelligence; I came up in the "Vulture" man-of-war for this effect, and was fetched by a boat from the ship to the beach. Being there, I was told that the approach of day would prevent my return, and that I must be concealed until the next night. I was in my regimentals, and had fairly risked my person.

Against my stipulation, my intention, and without my knowledge beforehand, I was conducted within one of your posts. Your Excellency may conceive my sensation on this occasion, and will imagine how much more must I have been affected by a refusal to reconduct me back the next night as I had been brought. Thus become a prisoner, I had to concert my escape. I quitted my uniform, and was passed another way in the night, without the American posts, to neutral ground, and informed I was beyond all armed parties, and left to press for New York. I was taken at Tarrytown by some volunteers.

Thus, as I have had the honour to relate, was I betrayed (being Adjutant-General of the British Army) into the vile condition of an enemy in disguise within your posts.

Having avowed myself a British officer, I have nothing to reveal but what relates to myself, which is true on the honour of an officer and a gentleman.

The request I have to make to your Excellency is, that in any rigor policy may dictate, a decency of conduct towards me may mark your actions on the grounds that though unfortunate I am branded with nothing dishonorable, as no motive could be mine but the service of my King, and as I was involuntarily an impostor.

It is no less, Sir, in a confidence of the generosity of your mind, than on account of your superior station, that I have chosen to importune you with this letter. I have the honour to be, with great respect, Sir, your Excellency's most obedient humble servant,

JOHN ANDRÉ, Adjutant-General

131

General Washington did not answer the Major's appeal but he fed the prisoner from his own table. Major André addressed one further letter to the General requesting that he not be hanged as a spy but honorably shot.

Sir:

Buoyed above the terror of death, by the consciousness of a life devoted to honorable pursuits and stained with no action that can give me remorse, I trust that the request I make to your Excellency at this serious period, and which is to soften my last moment, will not be rejected.

Sympathy toward a soldier will surely induce your Excellency and a military tribunal to adapt the mode of my death to the feelings of a man of honour.

Let me hope, Sir, that if aught in my character impresses you with esteem towards me, if aught in my misfortunes marks me as the victim of policy and not of resentment, I shall experience the operation of these feelings in your breast, by being informed that I am not to die on a gibbet.

JOHN ANDRÉ, Adj. Gen. to the British Army

André was hanged at Tappan, which is a village of Rockland County, New York. He was immediately made a hero and personal symbol. The revolutionaries could be proud of him since they too were British. The account of his last moments and the admirable manner in which he died are best taken from the Memoirs of General Heath, who was Colonial Commander of the Hudson River area at this time. We read in General Heath's diary:

October 2: Major André is no more among the living. I have just witnessed his exit. It was a tragical scene of the deepest interest. During his confinement and trial, he exhibited those proud and elevated sensibilities which designate greatness and dignity of mind. Not a murmur or a sigh ever escaped him, and the civilities and attentions bestowed on him were politely acknowledged.

Having left a mother and two sisters in England, he was heard to mention them in terms of the tenderest affection, and in his letter to Sir Henry Clinton, he recommends them to his particular attention.

The principal guard officer, who was constantly in the room with the prisoner, relates that when the hour of his execution was announced to him in the morning, he received it without emotion, and while all present were affected with silent gloom, he retained a firm countenance, with calmness and composure of mind. Observing his servant enter the room in tears, he exclaimed, "Leave me till you can show yourself more manly."

His breakfast being sent to him from the table of General Washington, which had been done every day of his confinement, he partook of it as usual, and having shaved and drest himself, he placed his hat on the table, and cheerfully said to the guard officers, "I am ready at any moment, gentlemen, to wait on you."

The fatal hour having arrived, a large detachment of troops was paraded, and an immense concourse of people assembled; almost all our general and field officers, excepting his Excellency and his staff, were present on horseback; melancholy and gloom pervaded all ranks, and the scene was affectingly awful. I was so near during the solemn march to the fatal spot, as to observe every moment, and share in every emotion which the sad scene was calculated to produce.

Major André walked from the stone house, in which he had been confined, between two of our subaltern officers, arm in arm; the eyes of the immense multitude were fixt on him, who, rising superior to the fears of death, appeared as if conscious of the dignity which he displayed.

He betrayed no want of fortitude, but retained a complacent smile on his countenance, and politely bowed to several gentlemen whom he knew, which was respectfully returned. It was his earnest desire to be shot, as being the mode of death most fitting to the feelings of a military man, and he had indulged the hope that his request would be granted.

At the moment, therefore, when suddenly he came in view of the gallows, he involuntarily started backward, and made a pause. "Why this emotion, sir," said an officer by his side. Instantly recovering his composure, he said, "I am reconciled to my death, but I detest the mode." While waiting and standing near the gallows, I observed some degree of trepidation; placing his foot on a stone, and rolling it over and choking in his throat, as if attempting to swallow.

So soon, however, as he perceived that things were in readiness, he stept quickly into the wagon, and at this moment he appeared to shrink, but instantly elevating his head with firmness, he said, "It will be but a momentary pang," and he took from his pocket two white handkerchiefs; the provost marshal with one loosely pinioned his arms, and with the other, the victim, after taking off his hat and stock, bandaged his own eyes with perfect firmness, which melted the hearts, and moistened the cheeks, not only of his servant, but of the throng of spectators.

When the rope was appended to the gallows, he slipped the noose over his head and adjusted it to his neck, without the assistance of the awkward executioner. Colonel Scammel now informed him that he had an opportunity to speak, if he desired it; he raised the handkerchief from his eyes and said, "I pray you to bear me witness that I meet my fate like a brave man."

The wagon being now removed from under him he was suspended and instantly expired; it proved indeed "but a momentary pang." He was drest in his royal regimentals and boots, and his remains, in the same dress, were placed in an ordinary coffin, and interred at the foot of the gallows; and the spot was consecrated by the tears of thousands. Thus died in the bloom of life, the accomplished Major André, the prize of the Royal Army.

An English newspaper of the time carried this editorial:

Many historians have been inclined to blame Washington for unnecessary severity in not acceding to the request of the prisoner (André), that he might be shot instead of hanged. We cannot agree with them: the ignominious death was decided upon by Washington—after much and anxious deliberation, and against his own feelings, which inclined to grant the prayer—as a strictly preventive punishment; and it had its effect. The social qualities and the letter of André, although they are always brought forward in his favor, do not extenuate but rather aggravate his crime, as they show that, whatever his moral principles may have been, he had the education of an English gentleman. If anything, his memory has been treated with too great leniency. If monuments are to be erected in Westminster Abbey to men of such lax morality, it is time for honesty to hide its head.

The conduct of Sir Henry Clinton, in receiving Arnold when he fled to the English ranks, and giving him a high command, is only in keeping with his countenance of the plot that cost André his life. Arnold, who seems to have been a miserable scoundrel, born to serve as a foil to the virtuous brightness of George Washington, might have redeemed his character by giving himself up in place of André, who was entrapped by Arnold's cowardice and over-caution; but such a piece of self-sacrifice never entered his head. A villain himself, he never believed in the success of the struggle of honest men, and his conduct after obtaining the protection of Sir Henry Clinton proves this beyond a doubt. Let him rest with all his British honours thick upon him.

Come all you brave Americans and unto me give ear,
I'll sing you now a ditty that will your spirits cheer,
Concerning a young gentleman who went to Tarrytown
Where he met a British officer, a man of high renown.

Then up stepped this young hero, John Paulding was
    his name,
"Oh, tell us where you're going, sir, and also whence
    you came."
"I bear the British flag, sir," of answer bold and gray,
"I have a pass that takes me through, I have no time
    to stay."

Then others came around him and bid him to dismount,
"Come tell us where you're going, give us a strict
    account."
Young Paulding said, "We are resolved that you shall
    ne'er pass by,"
And soon the evidence did prove, the prisoner was a spy.

He beggèd for his liberty, he pled for his discharge,
And often times he told them if they'd set him at large
"Here's all the gold and silver I have laid up in store,
But when I reach the city, I will send you ten times more."

"We scorn this gold and silver you have laid up in store,"
Then Ward and Paulding both did cry, "You need not
    send us more."
He saw that his conspiracy would soon be brought to
    light
He begged for pen and paper and he asked for to write.

The story came to Arnold, commanding at the Fort.
He callèd for "The Vulture" and sailèd for New York.

Now Arnold to New York had gone, a-fighting for
   his King
And left poor Major André on the gallows for to swing.

André was executed, he looked both meek and mild,
His face was fair and handsome and pleasantly he smiled.
It moved each eye with pity and every heart there bled,
And everyone wished him released and Arnold in
    his stead.

He was a man of honor, in Britain he was born
To die upon the gallows, most highly he did scorn.
And now his life has reached its end, so young and
    blooming still
In Tappan's quiet countryside, he sleeps upon the hill.

POETRY AND THE NEWS

"Give me the city desk poet any day who subordinates his rhyme to the matters of a fact," said Dr. Sam, "rather than the historian who romanticizes the facts of a matter."

Almost every major battle of the Revolution was celebrated in verse. The following rhyming summary of the Battle of Saratoga is from a newspaper account:

> Here followeth the direful fate
> Of Burgoyne and his army great
> Who so proudly did display
> The terrors of despotic sway
> His power and pride and many threats
> Have been brought low for fort'nate Gates
> To bend to the United States

British prisoners by Convention	2442
Foreigners by Contra-vention	2198
Tories sent across the Lake	1100
Burgoyne and his suite, in state	12
Sick and wounded, bruised and pounded Ne'er so much before confounded	528
Prisoners of war before Convention	400
Deserters come with kind intention	300

They lost at Bennington's great battle ⎱   1220
Where Stark's glorious arms did rattle ⎰
Kill'd in September and October   600
Ta'en by brave Brown, some drunk, some sober   413
Slain by high-famed Herkimer   300
On both flanks, on rear and van
Indians, suttlers, butchers, drovers,
Enough to crowd large plains all over
And those whom grim Death did prevent
From fighting against our continent;
And also those who stole away,   4413
Lest they down their arms should lay,
Abhorring that obnoxious day;
The whole make fourteen thousand men
Who may not with us fight again

                                  14,000

     This is a pretty just account
     Of Burgoyne's legion's whole amount,
     Who came across the Northern Lakes
     To desolate our happy States.
     Their brass cannons we have got all
     Fifty-six both great and small;
     And ten thousand stand of arms,
     To prevent all future harms.
     Among our prisoners there are
     Six generals, of fame most rare;
     Six members of their Parliament—
     Reluctantly they seem content;
     Three British lords and Lord Belcarras,
     Who came, our country free to harass.
     Two baronets, of high extraction,
     Were sorely wounded in action

And there was a broadside published to the melody of an
Irish ballad which is such an excellent description of the battle
itself, that we cannot resist reproducing it here.

THE BATTLE OF SARATOGA

Come unto me, ye heroes
And I the truth will tell
Concerning many a soldier
Who for his country fell.
Burgoyne, the King's commander
And cursèd Tory crew,
With Indians and Canadians
He up the Champlain flew.

He up the Champlain flew,
He up the Champlain flew,
With Indians and Canadians
He up the Champlain flew.

Before the Ticonderoga,
Full well both night and day
Their motions we observed
Before the bloody fray;
Burgoyne sent Baum to Bennington,
With Hessians there he went,
To plunder and to murder
Was fully their intent.

Was fully their intent,
Was fully their intent,
To plunder and to murder
Was fully their intent.

But little did they know then
With whom they had to deal.
It was not quite so easy
Our stores and stocks to steal.
Stark would give them only
A portion of his lead,

With half his crew ere sunset,
Baum lay among the dead.

The nineteenth of September,
The morning cool and clear,
Gates addressed the army
Each soldier's heart to cheer.
"Burgoyne," he cried, "advances,
But we will never fly,
But rather than surrender,
We'll fight him till we die!"

The seventh of October
They did capitulate,
Burgoyne and his proud army
We did our prisoners make.
And vain was their endeavor
Our men to terrify,
Though death was all around us,
Not one of us would fly!

Now here's a health to Herkimer
And our Commander Gates!
To Freedom and to Washington
Whom every Tory hates.
Likewise unto our Congress—
God grant it long to reign—
Our country, rights and justice
Forever to maintain.

SURRENDERING

Cornwallis, the last commander-in-chief of the British armies in America, lost the decisive and final battle of the American War for Independence at Yorktown. We have great insight on how things looked from his point of view in this his official report, dated October 20, 1781:

> I have the mortification to inform your excellency that I have been forced to give up the posts of York and Gloucester, and to surrender the troops under my command, by capitulation, on the 19th instant, as prisoners of war to the combined forces of America and France.
>
> I never saw this post in a very favorable light, but when I found I was to be attacked in it in so unprepared a state, by so powerful an army and artillery, nothing but the hopes of relief would have induced me to attempt its defense, for I would either have endeavored to escape to New York by rapid marches from the Gloucester side, immediately on the arrival of General Washington's troops at Williamsburg, or I would, not withstanding the disparity of numbers, have attacked them in the open field, where it might have been just possible that fortune would have favored the gallantry of the handful of troops under my command; but being assured by your Excellency's letters that every possible means would be tried by the navy and

army to relieve us, I could not think myself at liberty to venture upon either of these desperate attempts; therefore, after remaining for two days in a strong position in front of this place in hopes of being attacked, upon observing that the enemy were taking measures which could not fail of turning my left flank in a short time, and receiving on the second evening your letter of September 24th, informing me that the relief would sail about October 5th, I withdrew within the works on the night of September 29th, hoping by the labour and firmness of the soldiers to protract the defence until you could arrive. Everything was to be expected from the spirit of the troops, but every disadvantage attended their labour, as the works were to be continued under the enemy's fire, and our stock of entrenching tools, which did not much exceed four hundred when we began to work in the latter end of August, was now diminished . . .

Our numbers had been diminished by the enemy's fire, but particularly by sickness, and the strength and spirits of those in the works were much exhausted by the fatigue of constant watching and unremitting duty. Under all these circumstances I thought it would have been wanton and inhuman to the last degree to sacrifice the lives of this small body of gallant soldiers, who had ever behaved with so much fidelity and courage, by exposing them to an assault which, from the numbers and precautions of the enemy, could not fail to succeed. I therefore proposed to capitulate; and I have the honour to enclose to your Excellency the copy of the correspondence between General Washington and me.

Washington's orders to his troops at this time showed his tremendous sense of fairness. He said:

My brave fellows . . . let no shouting, no clamorous huzzahing increase their mortification. It is sufficient to us that we witness their humiliation. Posterity will huzzah for us.

143

This really deserves to stand beside the cherry-tree story.

Pleading illness as an excuse, Lord Cornwallis did not appear. His substitute, General O'Hara, rode toward Washington, removed his hat in salutation and prepared to give up his sword. He was referred to General Lincoln who received the sword and immediately handed it back. It is an interesting point that the English officers saluted the French officers as they passed but showed no such courtesy to the Americans in command. As the British soldiers laid down their arms, their band played a quaint old English melody, entitled, "The World's Turned Upside Down," which, when one examines the words shows a most unusually good-humored awareness from the defeated army:

> If buttercups buzz'd after the bee,
> If boats were on land, churches on sea,
> If ponies rode men, and if grass ate the cows,
> And cats should be chased into holes by the mouse,
> If all mamas sold their babies to the gypsies for
>   half a crown,
> If summer were spring, and the other way 'round,
> Then all the world would be upside down.

"Well, that's the way it goes," as my uncle Dr. Sam said when he wanted to end a discussion for which he had no final word.

A DELICATE MOMENT

Probably one of the most embarrassing meetings between countries was that between England and the newly-formed country, America. How does a mother country greet a rebellious colony that is now a country demanding equal status in the family of nations?

John Adams was sent to represent the United States at the Court of George III. The burden of this embarrassment was on both him and the king. Adams made a report of what happened.

We learn that the Marquis of Carmarthen instructed Adams in what was customary for a foreign minister. He was taken to the Court in the Marquis' coach where, with the other foreign representatives, he stood waiting to be received in the ante-chamber of the king's bedchamber.

He felt embarrassed that he was the focus of all eyes. The Swedish and Dutch ministers completely relieved him by conversing with him during his period of waiting. Finally, he found himself alone with His Majesty.

Adams made three bows, he tells us, one at the door, another halfway, and another before the presence—in accordance with the custom of the time. He then addressed His Majesty in the following words:

Sir: The United States of America have appointed me their

minister plenipotentiary to Your Majesty, and have directed me to deliver to Your Majesty this letter, which contains the evidence of it. It is in obedience to their express commands, that I have the honor to assure Your Majesty of their unanimous disposition and desire to cultivate the most friendly and liberal intercourse between Your Majesty's subjects and their citizens, and of their best wishes for Your Majesty's health and happiness, and for that of your royal family. The appointment of a minister from the United States to Your Majesty's Court will form an epoch in the history of England and of America. I think myself more fortunate than all my fellow citizens, in having the distinguished honor to be the first to stand in Your Majesty's royal presence in a diplomatic character; and I shall esteem myself the happiest of men, if I can be instrumental in recommending my country more and more to Your Majesty's royal benevolence, and of restoring an entire esteem, confidence, and affection, or, in better words, the old good nature and the old good humor between people, who, tho separated by an ocean, and under different governments, have the same language, a similar religion, and kindred blood.

I beg Your Majesty's permission to add, that altho I have some time before been entrusted by my country, it was never in my whole life in a manner so agreeable to myself.

We learn that the king listened to the speech with great emotion. Both men were apparently much affected, but Adams declared that the king spoke with even greater voice tremor. The king's pronunciation was distinct but he hesitated much between sentences. The king said:

Sir: The circumstances of this audience are so extraordinary, the language you have now held is so extremely proper, and the feelings you have discovered so justly adapted to the occasion, that I must say that I not only receive with pleasure the assurance of the friendly dispositions of the United States, but that I am very glad the choice has fallen upon you to be their minister. I wish you, sir, to believe, and that it may be understood in America, that I have done nothing in the late contest but what I thought myself indispensably bound to do, by the duty which I owed to my people. I will be very frank with you. I was the last to consent to the separation; but the separation having been made, and having become inevitable, I have always said, as I say now, that I would be the first to meet the friendship of the United States as an independent power. The moment I see such sentiments and language as yours prevail, and a disposition to give to this country the preference, that moment I shall say, let the circumstances of language, religion, and blood have their natural and full effect.

Mr. Adams thought from his conversation with the king that his residence in London would be less painful than anticipated. He suggested in his report that this exchange of conversation should be kept secret in America for the time being.

AMERICAN BEAUTIES—MALE

It is a matter of pride to contemporary Americans and Australians, that they are taller and heavier than the European stock from which they came. Apparently a Hessian officer found this to be true of Americans after the Battle of Saratoga in 1777. In a letter back home to Germany after General Gates had accepted the surrender of the British forces, he describes the appearance of "the Americans, who, for politeness sake, are no longer termed Rebels or Yankees":

We passed the enemy's encampment, in front of which all their regiments, as well as the artillery, were standing under arms. Not a man of them was regularly equipped. Each one had on the clothes which he was accustomed to wear in everyday life. No fault, however, could be found with their military appearance, for they stood in an erect and a soldierly attitude. All their muskets had bayonets attached to them, and their riflemen had rifles. They remained so perfectly quiet that we were utterly astounded. Not one of them made any attempt to speak to the man at his side; and all the men who stood in array before us were so slender, fine-looking, and sinewy, that it was a pleasure to look at them. Nor could we but wonder that Dame Nature had created such a handsome race! As to their height, dear brother, the men averaged from six to seven inches, according to Prussian measurement; and I assure you I am not telling an untruth when I state that men of eight to ten inches high were oftener to be seen than those of only five; and men of larger height were to be found in all the companies.

The reader should be assured that an American of from "six to seven inches" was, of course, 5 feet 6 to 5 feet 7 inches, and men "eight to ten inches" were 5 feet 8 to 5 feet 10, according to the Prussian terminology.

The writer concludes his praises of the Americans:

I am perfectly serious when I state that the men of English America are far ahead of those in the greater portion of Europe both as respects their beauty and stature.

Every American male should read this item if only to understand the natural pride that makes his purchase of hair tonics, consumption of vitamins and barbershop attendance so high. So it was and so it will be.

"ALL IS WELL"

During the night I am occasionally awakened by some rude noise of the New York City streets—a cry or scream of a woman—a gun—a siren. How much more pleasant to have heard the melodic reassurance of the town crier as described by John Melish in western Pennsylvania in 1811:

Again a day is past, and a step made nearer to our end; our time runs away, and the joys of Heaven are our reward.

The night watch repeated this sentence at eleven, twelve, one and two o'clock. At three o'clock, the time of their last round, they called:

Again a night is past and the morning is come; our time runs away, and the joys of Heaven are our reward.

42

SOME EIGHTEENTH-CENTURY EPITAPHS

AT BARNSTABLE, MASS.

Rev. Joseph Green, 1770, aet. 70

Think what the Christian minister should be,
You've then his character, for such was he.

AT ANDOVER, MASS.

John Abbot, 1793, aet. 90

Grass, smoke, a flower, a vapor, shade, a span,
Serve to illustrate the frail life of man;
And they, who longest live, survive to see
The certainty of death, of life and vanity.

The following is a copy of the epitaph written by Franklin upon himself, at the age of twenty-three, while a journeyman printer:

The Body
of
Benjamin Franklin, Printer,
(Like the cover of an old book,
Its contents torn out,
And stript of its lettering and gilding,)
Lies food for worms:
Yet the work itself shall not be lost,
For it will (as he believed) appear once more
In a new
And more beautiful edition
Corrected and amended
by
The Author.

ON AN IMPORTUNATE TAILOR

Here lies W. W.,
Who never more will trouble you, trouble you.

A SOUTH CAROLINA TRIBUTE TO DEPARTED WORTH

Here lies the boddy of Robert Gordin,
Mouth almighty and teeth ackordin,
Stranger tread lightly over this wonder,
If he opens his mouth, you are gone by thundr.

She lived a life of virtue, and died of the cholera morbus, caused by eating green fruit, in hope of a blessed immortality, at the early age of 21 years, 7 months and 16 days! Reader, "Go thou and do likewise."

IN MORETON CHURCHYARD

Here lies the bones of Roger Norton
Whose sudden death was oddly broght on:
Trying one day his corns to mow off!
The razor slipt and cut his toe off!
The toe—or, rather what it grew to—
An inflammation quickly flew to;
The part then took to mortifying,
Which was the cause of Roger's dying.

In Memory of William French, Who Was Shot at Westminster March ye 12th, 1775, by the hand of the Cruel Ministerial tools of George ye 3rd at the Courthouse at 11 o'clock at Night in the 22nd year of his age.

Here William French his Body lies,
For Murder his Blood for Vengeance Cries.
King George the third his Tory crew
that with a bawl his head Shot threw,
For Liberty and his Countrys Good
he Lost his Life his Dearest blood.

On the death of General Wolfe, a premium was offered for the best epitaph on that officer. One of the candidates for the

153

prize sent a poem, of which the following stanza is a specimen:

> He marched without dread or fears,
> At the head of his bold grenadiers;
> And what was more remarkable—nay, *very particular*—
> He climbed up rocks that were perpendicular.

AN EARLY ASSEMBLY LINE

We are so accustomed to mass production, turning out thousands of objects exactly alike, that we find it hard to think of a time when everything was made separately and by hand. It was a great innovation when firearms were made in such a way that parts belonging to one could be used interchangeably with parts belonging to any other.

In 1785, Thomas Jefferson discovered that the French government had established a large factory for this purpose. In a letter to John Hay, he called this to his attention:

> . . . As yet, the inventor has only completed the lock of the musket, on this plan. He will proceed immediately to have the barrel, stock, and other parts, executed in the same way. Supposing it might be useful in the United States, I went to the workman. He presented me the parts of fifty locks taken to pieces, and arranged in compartments. I put several together myself, taking pieces at hazard as they came to hand, and they fitted in the most perfect manner. The advantages of this, when arms need repair, are evident. He effects it by tools of his own contrivance, which, at the same time, abridge the work, so that he thinks he shall be able to furnish the musket two livres cheaper than the common price. But it will be two or three years before he will be able to furnish any quantity. I mention it now, as it may have an influence on the plan for furnishing our magazines with this arm.

AMERICA, THE MAGNET

After the Revolutionary War, the idea that America was the place to get rich quickly prevailed all over Europe as it had not since the Spanish conquistadores had come in search of wealth.

In London, in 1795, Benjamin Franklin was moved to write a pamphlet, *Information to Those Who Would Remove to America,* in which he attempted to discourage those who thought America a place to get rich quickly without work:

> The truth is, that, though there are . . . few people so miserable as the poor of Europe, there are also very few that in America would be called rich. It is rather a general happy mediocrity that prevails. Much less is it advisable for a person to go thither who has no other quality to recommend him than his birth. In Europe it has, indeed, its value, but it is a commodity that cannot be carried to a worse market than to that of America, where people do not enquire, concerning a stranger, *What is he,* but *What can he do?* In short, America is the land of labour, and by no means what the English call *Lubberland,* and the French, *Pays de Cocagne,* where the streets are said to be paved with half-peck loaves, the houses tiled with pancakes, and where the fowls fly about ready roasted, crying, *come, eat me.*

Others wrote advice for the would-be emigrants. One Thomas Cooper in his *Some Information Representing America,* published in London in 1795, explained what it meant to be a farmer in the new country:

> Nor is the term "farmer" synonymous with the same word in England. With you it means a tenant holding of some lord, paying much in rent, and much in tythes, and much in taxes: an inferior rank in life, occupied by persons of inferior manners and education. In America a farmer is a landowner, paying no rent, no tythes, and few taxes, equal in rank to any other rank in the state, having a voice in the appointment of his legislators, and a fair chance, if he deserves it, of becoming one himself. In fact, nine-tenths of the legislators of America are farmers.

THE EDUCATION OF CHILDREN: 1790

In early days, as now, much attention was given by educators
to the cultivation of children's minds. About 1790, we find an
alphabet book published for the development of the interests
and minds of the young:

A In Adam's fall, we sinnèd all.
B Thy life to mend, God's Book attend.
C The cat doth play, and after slay.
D A dog will bite a thief at night.
E The eagle's flight is out of sight.
F The idle fool is whipt at school.
G As runs the glass, man's life doth pass.
H My book and heart shall never part.
I [was omitted]
J Job feels the rod, yet blesses God.
K Proud Korak's troop was swallowed up.
L The lion bold the lamb doth hold.
M The moon give light in time of night.
N Nightingales sing in time of spring.
O The royal oak it was the tree that sav'd His
　　Royal Majesty.
P Peter denies his Lord and cries.
Q Queen Esther comes in royàl state to save the
　　Jews from dismal fate.

R   Rachel doth mourn for her first-born.
S   Samuel anoints whom God appoints.
T   Time cuts down all, both great and small.
U   Uriah's beauteous wife made David seek his life.
V   [was omitted]
W   Whales in the sea, God's voice obey.
X   Xerxes the Great did die and so must you and I.

It was at this time also that the Ten Commandments were put into short and easy rhymes for children:

> Thou shalt have no more Gods but me,
> Before no idol bend thy knee;
> Take not the name of God in vain,
> Dare not the Sabbath Day profane.
> Give both thy parents honor due,
> Take heed that thou no murder do.
> Abstain from words and deed unclean,
> Steal not, though thou be poor and mean.
> Make not a wilful lie, no love it;
> What is thy neighbor's, dare not covet.

"I can't swallow that," Dr. Sam Icle Ivanhoe belched in spiritual dyspepsia. "Fancy paring the words of the Almighty into an alphabet soup." He gave me the one hush-puppy remaining on his plate. "Fill your mouth with this . . . and fill your heart with the hymn I'm about to sing you." And he sang a hymn of his own creating:

> Press Upward, Press Upward,
> God is in view.
> A host of bright angels is watching
> O'er you.

159

MOTHER GOOSE A BAD INFLUENCE

Abigail Adams, wife of John Adams, was in favor of the moralizing purpose of most of the contemporary books for children. On the other hand she, with others interested in children's education, frowned upon nonsense like Mother Goose. The continual and continuing popularity of Mother Goose seems a good argument against their precepts.

Mrs. Adams wrote to a friend in November, 1790, from Philadelphia:

Keep in mind the great importance of first principles, and the necessity of instilling the precepts of morality very early into their minds. Youth is so imitative, that it catches at everything. I have a great opinion of Dr. Watts' "Moral Songs for Children." They are adapted to the capacities, and they comprehend all the social and relative duties of life. They impress the young mind with the ideas of the Supreme Being, as their creator, benefactor, and preserver. They teach brotherly love, sisterly affection, and filial respect and reverence. I do not know any book so well calculated for the early period of life; and they may be made as pleasant to them, by the method of instructing, as a hundred little stories, which are taught them, containing neither a rule of life, nor a sentiment worth retaining, such as "Jack and Jill," and "Little Jack Horner." As a trial of their memory, and a practice for their tongues, these may be useful, but no other way.

JEFFERSON ON THE INDIAN PROBLEM

Thomas Jefferson, during his long career as a member of our early American government, displayed many changing attitudes toward the Indians as he was faced by different problems. In 1786, he wrote from Paris to a Mr. Hawkins:

. . . . The attention which you pay to their (the Indians') rights does you great honor, as the want of that is a principal source of dishonor to the American character. The two principles on which our conduct toward the Indians should be founded, are justice and fear. After the injuries we have done them, they cannot love us, which leaves us no alternative but that of fear to keep them from attacking us. But justice is what we should never lose sight of, and in time it may recover their esteem. . . .

In 1791, writing from Philadelphia to Mr. Charles Carroll, we find Jefferson deprecating the use of American fighting men as a means of controlling the Indians. At this time, he wrote:

Our news from the westward is disagreeable. Constant murders committed by the Indians, and their combination threatens to be more and more extensive. I hope we shall give them a thorough drubbing this summer, and then change our tomahawk into a golden chain of friendship.

The most economical as well as most humane conduct toward them is to bribe them into peace, and to retain them in peace by eternal bribes. The expedition this year would have served for presents on the most liberal scale for one hundred years; nor shall we otherwise ever get rid of an army, or of our debt. The least rag of Indian depredation will be an excuse to raise troops for those who love to have troops, and for those who think that a public debt is a good thing.

Always interested in the Indian question, Jefferson made a continuous study of Indian languages and was in constant communication with men in various parts of the country, requesting information from them with respect to the Indian tongues of their areas. In 1803, during his Presidency, he was faced with the practical problem of what to do about the Indians who were already being pushed westward. There was already talk about Indian reservations and here is his attitude toward the matter, expressed in a letter dated at Washington, addressed to Colonel Hawkins in February, 1803:

I consider the business of hunting as already become insufficient to furnish clothing and subsistence to the Indians. The promotion of agriculture, therefore, and household manufacture, are essential in their preservation, and I am disposed to aid and encourage it liberally. In truth, the ultimate point of rest and happiness for them is to let our settlements and theirs meet and blend together, to intermix, and become one people. Incorporating themselves with us as citizens of the United States, this is what the natural progress of things will, of course, bring on, and it will be better to promote than to retard it. Surely it will be better for them to be identified with us, and preserved in the occupation of their lands, than be exposed to the many casualties which may endanger them while a separate people. I have little doubt but that your reflections must have led you to view the various ways in which their history may terminate, and to see that this is the one most for their happiness. And we have already had an application from a settlement of Indians to become citizens of the United States. It is possible, perhaps probable, that this idea may be so novel as that it might shock the Indians, were it even hinted to them. Of course, you will keep it for your own reflection; but, convinced of its soundness, I feel it consistent with pure morality to lead them towards it, to familiarize them to the idea. . . .

Jefferson was more just than smart in his dealings with the Indians, insisting that they be paid for lands which they sold or leased. He made these two noteworthy addresses on the subject while he was President, the first to the Choctaw Nation in 1805 and the second to the Cherokee chiefs who visited Washington in 1806:

My Children—I learn with great satisfaction that you have leased to us three stations of one mile square each on the road from Chickasaws to Natchez, and one of the Pearl River; and you desire me to send you a paper under my own hand to show to your warriors that these lands are not sold but lent. I now accordingly declare that the property in those lands remains in your nations, that they are lent to us for a rent of four hundred pounds weight of powder annually, and that your nation has a right to take them back at their pleasure; and this paper now signed by my own hand will be evidence of these things to future generations. We will, according to your desire, settle but one white family on each section, and take care that they conduct themselves peaceably and friendly toward you; or being made known to me that they do otherwise they shall be removed.

They will be placed there merely for the accommodation of our paper carriers and travelers.

My children, you have asked whether I did not promise to send you ploughs to enable you to improve in husbandry? I did promise it and immediately sent the ploughs; but by a mistake in forwarding them, they were delayed some time before we knew of it. You must, however, have received them before this time.

You ask if I did not promise to send your deputation ten rifles for yourselves and other deserving warriors? I did not promise it. You said they would be acceptable, but I said nothing in reply. But although I did not promise, yet to show my good will to you, I will send the rifles.

You ask if we will allow commissions to you according to your rank and medals and commissions to such chiefs as you may appoint to assist in the government of your country? It has not been a custom with us to give commissions to our friends among the red men; and it is a new thing. We will take it into consideration. We wish to do what is agreeable to you, if we find we can do it with prudence.

We shall be willing to give medals to a certain number of distinguished chiefs who aid you in the government of your country, and who manifest dispositions to preserve peace and friendship between your nation and ours. We wish you, therefore, to recommend such to us.

My children, persevere in your friendship to the United States. We will never injure you nor permit you to be injured by any white people, and we trust you will take care that none of our people are injured by yours. Encourage among you the cultivation of the earth, raising of cattle, spinning and weaving, and we will assist you in it. With plenty of food and clothing you will raise many children, multiply, be strong and happy. May the Great Spirit protect and prosper you in all your just pursuits. Farewell.

My Friends and Children, chiefly of the Cherokee Nation:—Having now finished our business and finished it I hope to mutual satisfaction, I cannot take leave of you without expressing the satisfaction I have received from your visit. I see with my own eyes that the endeavors we have been making to encourage and lead you in the way of improving your situation have not been unsuccessful; it has been like grain sown in good ground, producing abundantly. You are becoming farmers, learning the use of the plough and the hoe, enclosing your grounds and employing that labor in their cultivation which you formerly employed in hunting and in war; and I see handsome specimens of cotton cloth raised, spun and woven by yourselves. You are also raising cattle and hogs for your good, and horses to assist your labors. Go on, my children, in the same way and be assured the further you advance in it the happier and more respectable you will be.

Our brethren, whom you have happened to meet here from the West and Northwest, have enabled you to compare your situation now with what it was formerly. They also make the comparison, and they see how far you are ahead of them, and seeing what you are they are encouraged to do as you have done. You will find your next wants to be mills to grind your corn, which by relieving your women from the loss of time in beating it into meal, will enable them to spin and weave more. When a man has enclosed and improved his farm, builds a good house on it and raises plentiful stocks of animals, he will wish when he dies that these things shall go to his wife and children, whom he loves more than he does his other relations, and for whom he will work with pleasure during his life. You will, therefore, find it necessary to establish laws for this. When a man has property, earned by his own labor, he will not like to see another come and take it from him because he happens to be stronger, or else to defend it by spilling blood. You will find it necessary then to appoint good men, as judges, to decide contests between man and man, according to reason and to the rules you shall establish. If you wish to be aided by our counsel and experience in these things we shall always be ready to assist you with our advice.

My children, it is unnecessary for me to advise you

against spending all your time and labor in warring with and destroying your fellow men, and wasting your own members. You already see the folly and iniquity of it. Your young men, however, are not yet sufficiently sensible of it. Some of them cross the Mississippi to go and destroy people who have never done them an injury. My children, this is wrong and must not be; if we permit them to cross the Mississippi to war with the Indians on the other side of that river, we must let those Indians cross the river to take revenge on you. I say again, this must not be. The Mississippi now belongs to us. It must not be a river of blood. It is now the water path along which all our people of Natchez, St. Louis, Indiana, Ohio, Tennessee, Kentucky and the western parts of Virginia and Pennsylvania are constantly passing with their property, to and from New Orleans. Young men going to war are not easily restrained. Finding our people on the river they will rob them, perhaps kill them. This would bring on a war between us and you. It is better to stop this in time by forbidding your young men to go across the river to make war. If they go to visit or to live with the Cherokees on the other side of the river we shall not object to that. That country is ours. We will permit them to live in it.

My children, this is what I wished to say to you. To go on in learning to cultivate the earth and to avoid war. If any of your neighbors injure you, our beloved men whom we place with you will endeavor to obtain justice for you and we will support them in it. If any of your bad people injure your neighbors, be ready to acknowledge it and to do them justice. It is more honorable to repair a wrong than to persist in it. Tell all your chiefs, your men, women and children, that I take them by the hand and hold it fast. That I am their father, wish their happiness and well-being, and am always ready to promote their good.

My children, I thank you for your visit and pray to the Great Spirit who made us all and planted us all in this land to live together like brothers that He will conduct you safely to your homes, and grant you to find your families and your friends in good health.

Consistent with Jefferson's beliefs as to how the Indians should be treated, we find him sending this advice from Monticello in 1808 to his Secretary of War, Henry Dearborn, at a time when the Sacs and Foxes of Illinois were supposed to have murdered one white man:

I hope the Governor will be able to settle with the Sacs and Foxes without war, to which, however, he seems too much committed. If we had gone to war for every hunter or trader killed, and murderer refused, we should have had general and constant war. The process to be followed, in my opinion, when a murder has been committed, is first to demand the murderer, and not regarding a first refusal to deliver, give time and press it. If perseveringly refused, recall all traders, and interdict commerce with them, until he be delivered. I believe this would rarely fail in producing the effect desired; and we have seen that, by steadily following this line, the tribes become satisfied of our moderation, justice, and friendship to them, and become firmly attached to us. The want of time to produce these dispositions in the Indians west of the Mississippi, has been the cause of the Kansas, the Republican, the Great and the Wolf Panics, the Matas, and Poncaras, adhering to the Spanish interest against us. But if we use forebearance, and open commerce for them, they will come to, and give us time to attach them to us. The factories proposed on the Missouri and Mississippi, as soon as they can be in activity, will have more effect than as many armies. It is on their interests we must rely for their friendship, and not on their fears.

AN INDIAN'S WHITE WIFE

Many women were captured by the Indians and held in slavery and many of these were actually wed to their captors by Indian custom. There is one narrative by a Mrs. Mary Jamison, in which she recounts why she was satisfied to live with the Indians and remain with them. She had obviously found a good way of life:

I had then been with the Indians four summers and four winters, and had become so far accustomed to their mode of living, habits, dispositions, that my anxiety to get away, to be set at liberty, and leave them, had almost subsided. With them was my home; my family was there, and there I had many friends to whom I was warmly attached in consideration of the favors, affection and friendship with which they had uniformly treated me, from the time of my adoption. Our labor was not severe; and that of one year was exactly similar, in almost every respect, to that of the others, without that endless variety that is to be observed in the common labor of the white people. Notwithstanding the Indian women have all the fuel and bread to procure, and the cooking to perform, their task is probably not harder than that of white women, who have those articles provided for them; and their cares certainly are not half as numerous, nor as great. In the summer season, we planted, tended and harvested our corn, and generally had all our children with us; but had no master to oversee or drive us, so that we could work as leisurely as we pleased. We had no ploughs on the Ohio; but performed the whole process of planting and hoeing with a small tool that resembled, in some respect, a hoe with a very short handle.

Our cooking consisted in pounding our corn into samp or hominy, boiling the hominy, making now and then a cake and baking it in the ashes, and in boiling or roasting our venison. As our cooking and eating utensils consisted of a hominy block and pestle, a small kettle, a knife or two, and a few vessels of bark and wood, it required but little time to keep them in order for use.

Spinning, weaving, sewing, stocking knitting, and the like, are arts which have never been practised in the Indian tribes generally. After the Revolutionary War, I learned to sew, so that I could make my own clothing after a poor fashion; but the other domestic arts I have been wholly ignorant of, since my captivity. In the season of hunting, it is our business, in addition to our cooking, to bring home the game that was taken by the Indians, dress it, and carefully preserve the eatable meat, and prepare or dress the skins. Our clothing was fastened together with strings of deer skin, and tied on with the same.

49

SOME NINETEENTH-CENTURY JOKES
TO TELL ONE'S FRIENDS

Two lawyers when a knotty case was o'er,
Shook hands, and were as friendly as before;
"Zounds!" said the client. "I would fain know how
You can be friends, who were such foes just now?"
"Thou fool!" said one. "We lawyers, though so keen,
Like shears, ne'er cut ourselves, but what's between."

Adam laid down and slept;—and from his side
A woman in her magic beauty rose;
Dazzled and charmed, he called that woman bride,
And his first sleep became his last repose.

"Marriage, not mirage, Jane, here in your letter:
With your education, you surely know better."
Quickly spoke my young wife, while I sat in confusion,
" 'Tis quite correct, Thomas: they're each an illusion."

Rusticus wrote a letter to his love,
And filled it full of warm and keen desire;
He hoped to raise a flame, and so he did:
The lady put his nonsense in the fire.

PIRATE LAW

The heyday of piracy was the early nineteenth century. The pirates, although they were outside the law of most peoples, lived in obedience to a definite set of rules which they established themselves. For the most part the rules were drawn up in writing. Every member of the particular crew, assigned to the ship, signed the document. So that no one named should come first and thus be more responsible than any others, the document was signed in Round Robin. That is, all the signatures were written around the edge of the page, one following on the tail of the other. Here is an example of the Articles of Agreement on such document:

1. Every man has a vote in affairs of moment, has equal title to the fresh provisions, or strong liquor, at any time seized and may use them at pleasure, unless a scarcity makes it necessary for the good of all to vote a retrenchment.
2. Every man to be called fairly in turn by list on board of prizes because (over and above their proper share) they are allowed a shift of clothes. But if one defraud the company to the value of one dollar, in plate, jewels or money, the punishment is marooning. If robbery takes place between two crewmen the guilty one shall have his nose and ears slit and be set ashore not on some inhabited place but where he shall surely suffer hardship.

3. No person shall game at cards or dice for money at sea.

4. The lights and candles shall be put out at eight o'clock at night. If any remain still inclined for drinking they shall do so on the open deck.

5. All shall keep their firelocks, pistols and cutlass clean and fit for service.

6. No women allowed. If any man be found carrying one of the sex to sea, disguised, he is to suffer death.

7. Desertion of the ship or quitting quarters in battle is punished by death or marooning.

8. No striking another on board ship. Every man's quarrel shall be ended on shore, at sword and pistol; thus: The quartermaster, failing reconciliation, shall accompany both ashore with such assistance as he sees fit. The disputants are set back to back at twenty paces distance. At the command they turn and fire immediately (or else the pistol is knocked from their hand). If both miss, they come to their cutlasses.

9. No man shall talk of breaking up their way of living until each has shared 1,000 pounds. If any man should lose a limb or become a cripple in the common service, he shall have 800 dollars out of the public stock, and for lesser hurts proportionally.

10. The captain and quartermaster shall receive two shares in a prize. The sailing master, boatswain, and gunner, one share and one half. Other officers, one and one quarter. Sailors, one.

EMIGRANTS ON A NEW SHORE

The desolate wilderness which the new emigrant faced when he arrived at his destination in early nineteenth-century America was most masterly put by that master of fiction, Charles Dickens. He watched an emigrant family go ashore on one of the river banks in Pennsylvania:

Five men, as many women, and a little girl. All their worldly goods are a bag, a large chest and an old chair: one, old, high-backed, rush-bottomed chair; a solitary settler in itself. They are rowed ashore in the boat, while the vessel stands a little off awaiting its return, the water being shallow. They are landed at the foot of a high bank, on the summit of which are a few log cabins, attainable only by a long winding path. It is growing dusk; but the sun is very red, and shines in the water and on some of the treetops, like fire.

The men get out of the boat first; help out the women; take out the bag, the chest, the chair; bid the rowers "good-bye"; and shove the boat off for them. At the first plash of the oars in the water, the oldest woman of the party sits down in the old chair, close to the water's edge, without speaking a word. None of the others sit down, though the chest is large enough for many seats. They all stand where they landed, as if stricken into stone; and look after the boat. So they remain, quite still and silent: the old woman and her old chair, in the centre; the bag and chest upon the shore, without anybody heeding them: all eyes fixed upon the boat. It comes alongside, is made fast, the men jump on board, the engine is put in motion, and we go hoarsely on again. There they stand yet, without the motion of a hand. I can see them through my glass, when, in the distance and increasing darkness, they are mere specks to the eye: lingering there still: the old woman in the old chair, and all the rest about her: not stirring in the least degree. And thus I slowly lose them.

A GOUGING MATCH, VIRGINIA, 1806

Fighting was one of the major amusements of the frontier. Thomas Ashe, an Irishman, visited Charleston, Virginia, in 1806 and witnessed a ruckus. It all began with a variety of opinion "regarding the outcome of a horse race. . . ."

Umpires were called in; their judgment was rejected, and a kind of general battle ensued. This affray over, the quarrel took a smaller circle, confined to two individuals, a Virginian by birth, and a Kentuckian by adoption. A ring was formed, and the mob demanded whether they proposed to fight fair, or to rough and tumble. The latter mode was preferred. Perhaps you do not exactly understand the distinction of these terms. Fight fair, however, is much in the English manner; and here, as there, anything foul requires interference; but when the parties rough and tumble, neither the populace nor individuals are to intermeddle or hinder either combatant from tearing or rending the other on the ground, or in any other situation. You startle at the words *tear* and *rend*, and again do not understand me. You have heard these terms I allow applied to beasts of prey, and carnivorous animals; and your humanity cannot conceive them applicable to men; it nevertheless is so, and the fact will not permit me the use of any less expressive term. Let me proceed. Bulk and bone were in favour of the Kentuckian; science and craft in that of the Virginian. The former promised himself victory from his power, the latter from his science. Very few rounds had taken place, or fatal blows given, before the Virginian contracted his whole form, drew up his arms to his face, with his hands nearly closed in a conclave, by the fingers being bent to the full extension of the flexors, and summoning up all his energy for one act of desperation, pitched himself into the bosom of his opponent. Before the effect of this could be ascertained, the sky was rent by the shouts of the multitude; and I could learn that the Virginian had expressed as much beauty and skill in his retraction and bound, as if he had been bred in a menagerie, and practised action and attitude among panthers and wolves. The shock received by the Kentuckian, and the want of breath, brought him instantly to the ground. The Virginian never lost his hold, like those bats of the South who never quit the subject on which they fasten till they taste blood, he kept his knees on his enemy's body; fixing his claws in his hair, and his thumbs on his eyes, gave them an instantaneous start from their sockets. The sufferer roared aloud, but uttered no complaint. The citizens again shouted with joy; and bets of three to one were offered on the Virginian. The Kentuckian not being able to disentangle his adversary from his face, adopted a new mode of warfare; and, in imitation of the serpent which crushes such creatures to death as it proposes for its food, he extended his arms around the Virginian, and hugged him into closer contact with his huge body. The latter disliking this, cast loose the hair and convex eyes of his adversary, when both, folded together like bears in an embrace, rolled several turns over each other. The acclamations increased, and bets run that the Kentuckian "would give out," that is, after being mutilated and deprived of his eyes, ears, and nose, he would cry for mercy and aid. The public were not precisely right. Some daemon interposed for the biggest monster; he got his enemy under him, and in an instant snapped off his nose so close to his face that no manner of projection remained. The little Virginian made one further effort, and fastening on the under lip of his mutilator tore it over the chin. The Kentuckian at length *gave out*, on which the people carried off the victor, and he preferring a triumph to a doctor, who came to cicatrize his face, suffered himself to be chaired round the ground as the champion of the times, and the first *rougher and tumbler*. The poor wretch, whose eyes were started from their spheres, and whose lip refused its office, returned to the town, to hide his impotence and get his countenance repaired.

After winning this fight, Thomas Ashe had "had sufficient of the sports of the day," and returned to his inn to report the affair to his Quaker friend.

He was afflicted, but by no means surprised at the news I brought him, and informed me further, that such doings were common, frequently two or three times a week; and that twice a year, or at the spring and fall races, then continued for fourteen days without interruption, aided by the licentious and profligate of all the neighbouring States. As to the savage practice of fighting in the manner of wild beasts, my host entertained no hopes whatever of ever seeing it put down. It might be called a national taste, which the laws appeared afraid to violate; and therefore it reared its head above authority. Few nights elapsed without the exhibition of this new gymnastic; few mornings appeared that did not bring to day a friend or acquaintance with the loss of an eye or the mutilation of half his features.

THE FASHION FOR WOMEN

Mrs. Trollope could find no more virtue in the dress of the American woman than she found in American food or customs in general. On the other hand, not much later, one James Buckingham, perhaps because he was a man, found the American woman more than acceptable.

Here they are—a woman's and a man's point of view. First, Mrs. Trollope:

The ladies have strange ways of adding to their charms. They powder themselves immoderately, face, neck, and arms, with pulverized starch; the effect is indescribably disagreeable by daylight, and not favorable at any time. They are also most unhappily partial to false hair, which they wear in surprising quantities; this is the more to be lamented as they generally have very fine hair of their own. I suspect this fashion to arise from an indolent mode of making their toilet, and from accomplished ladies' maids not being very abundant; it is less trouble to append a bunch of waving curls here, there, and everywhere, than to keep their native tresses in perfect order.

Though the expense of the ladies' dress greatly exceeds, in proportion to their general style of living, that of the ladies of Europe, it is very far (excepting in Philadelphia) from being in good taste. They do not consult the seasons in the colours or in the style of their costume; I have often shivered at seeing a young beauty picking her way through the snow with a pale rose-colored bonnet, set on the very top of her head: I knew one young lady whose pretty little ear was actually frost-bitten from being thus exposed. They never wear muffs or boots, and appeared extremely shocked at the sight of comfortable walking shoes and cotton stockings, even when they have to step to their sleighs over ice and snow. I must say in their excuse, however, that they have, almost universally, extremely pretty feet. They do not walk well, nor, in fact, do they ever appear to advantage when in movement. I know not why this should be, for they have abundance of French dancing-masters among them, but somehow or other it is the fact. I fancied I could often trace a mixture of affectation and of shyness in their little mincing unsteady step, and the ever-changing position of the hands. They do not dance well; perhaps I should rather say they do not look well when dancing; lovely as their faces are, they cannot, in a position that exhibits the whole person, atone for the want of tournure, and for the universal defect in the formation of the bust, which is rarely full, or gracefully formed.

And now, from Mr. Buckingham:

The women far exceed the men in the costliness of their dresses and in the gayety of their walking apparel. There is perhaps no city in the world in which so many expensively dressed ladies may be seen walking or shopping, as on a fine morning may be met with in Broadway. Rich and bright-colored silks, satins, and other similarly costly materials, with ermine-lined cloaks and the most expensive furs; white, pink, and blue satin bonnets, with ostrich feathers and flowers of the first quality, are worn by all who assume to be genteel or rank in the class of ladies, and the

179

whole force of the wardrobe seems to be exhausted in the walking costume.

The women, moreover, are much handsomer than the men. They are almost uniformly good-looking; the greater number are what would be called in England "pretty women," which is something between good-looking and handsome, in the nice distinctions of beauty. This uniformity extends also to their figures, which are almost universally slender and of good symmetry. Very few large or stout women are seen, and none that we could call masculine. A more than usual degree of feminine delicacy, enhanced by the general paleness of complexion and slightness of figure, is particularly characteristic of American females; and the extreme respect and deference shown to them everywhere by men has a tendency to increase that delicacy, by making them more dependent on the attention and assistance of others than English ladies of the same class usually are.

PARODY ON THE DECLARATION
OF INDEPENDENCE

In North Carolina a tavern keeper, having grown rich, grew very careless; and so offended the lawyers, by whom his house had for years been filled, that with one accord they forsook him, leaving behind them the following parody on the Declaration of Independence:

When, in the course of human events, it becomes necessary for a half-hungry, half-fed, imposed-on set of men, to dissolve the bonds of landlord and boarder, a decent respect for the opinions of mankind requires that they should declare the causes which have impelled them to separation.

We hold these truths to be self-evident: that all men are created with mouths and stomachs; and they are endowed by their creator with certain inalienable rights; among which is, that no man shall be compelled to starve out of mere compliance to a landlord; and that every man has a right to fill his stomach and wet his whistle with the best that's going.

The history of the present landlord of the White Lion, is a history of repeated insults, exactions, and injuries, all having in direct object the establishment of absolute tyranny over their stomachs and throats. To prove this, let facts be submitted to a candid world.

He has refused to keep any thing to drink but bald-faced whiskey.

He has refused to set upon his table for dinner any thing but turnip soup, with a little tough beef and sourcrout, which are not wholesome and necessary for the public good.

He has refused to let his only servant, blink-eyed Joe, put more than six grains of coffee to one gallon of water.

He has turned loose a multitude of mosquitoes to assail us in the peaceful hours of the night and eat our substance.

He has kept up, in our beds and bedsteads, standing armies of merciless savages, with their scalping knives and tomahawks, whose rule of warfare is undistinguished destruction.

He has excited domestic insurrection among us, by taking bitters before breakfast, and making his wife and servant do the same before dinner, whereby there is often the deuce to pay.

He has waged cruel war against nature herself, by feeding our horses with broom-straw, and carrying them off to drink where swine refused to wallow.

He has protected one-eyed Joe in his villainy, in the robbery of our jugs, by pretending to give him a mock trial, after sharing with him the spoil.

He has cut off the trade from foreign port, and brought in his own bald-faced whiskey, when we had sent him to buy better liquor abroad; and, with a perfidy scarcely paralleled in the most barbarous ages, he has been known to drink our foreign spirits, and fill up our bottles with his own dire potions.

He has imposed taxes upon us to an enormous amount, without our consent, and without any rule but his own arbitrary will and pleasure.

A landlord whose character is thus marked by every act

which may define a tyrant and a master, is unfit to keep a boarding-house for Cherokee Indians.

Nor have we been wanting in our attention to Mrs. B. and Miss Sally. We have appealed to their native justice and magnanimity—we have conjured them to alter a state of things which would inevitably interrupt our connexion and correspondence. They, too, have been deaf to the voice of justice. We are, therefore, constrained to hold all three of these parties alike inimical to our well-being, and regardless of our comfort.

We therefore make this solemn declaration of our final separation from our former landlord, and cast our defiance in his teeth.

A LITTLE-KNOWN POEM OF 1806

TABITHA TOWZER
By Thomas G. Fessenden

Miss Tabitha Towzer is fair,
  No guinea pig ever was neater;
Like a hakmatack slender and spare,
  And sweet as a musk-squash or sweeter.

Miss Tabitha Towzer is sleek,
  When dress'd in her pretty new tucker,
Like an otter that paddles the creek,
  In quest of a mud-pout or sucker.

Her forehead is smooth as a tray,
  Ah! smoother than that on my soul,
And turned, as a body may say,
  Like a delicate neat wooden bowl.

To what shall I liken her hair,
  As straight as a carpenter's line,
For similes sure must be rare,
  When we speak of a nymph so divine.

Not the head of a Nazarite seer,
    That never was shaven or shorn,
Nought equals the locks of my dear,
    But the silk of an ear of green corn.

My dear has a beautiful nose,
    With a sled-runner crook in the middle,
Which one would be led to suppose
    Was meant for the head of a fiddle.

Miss Tabby has two pretty eyes,
    Glass buttons show never so bright;
Their love-lighted lustre outvies
    The lightning-bug's twinkle by night.

And oft with a magical glance,
    She makes in my bosom a pother,
When leering politely askance,
    She shuts one and winks with the other.

The lips of my charmer are sweet,
    As a hogshead of maple molasses;
And the ruby-red tint of her cheek
    The gill of a salmon surpasses.

No teeth like hers ever were seen,
    Nor ever described in a novel;
Of a beautiful kind of pea-green,
    And shaped like a wooden-shod shovel.

Her fine little ears you would judge,
    Were wings of a bat in perfection;
A dollar I never should grudge
    To put them in Peale's grand collection.

185

Description must fail in her chin;
   At least till our language is richer;
Much fairer than ladle of tin,
   Or beautiful brown earthen pitcher.

So pretty a neck, I'll be bound,
   Never join'd head and body together,
Like nice crook'd-neck'd squash on the ground,
   Long whiten'd by winter-like weather.

Should I set forth the rest of her charms,
   I might, by some phrase that's improper,
Give modesty's bosom alarms,
   Which I wouldn't do for a copper.

Should I mention her gait or her air,
   You might think I intended to banter;
She moves with more grace you would swear,
   Than a founder'd horse forc'd to a canter.

She sang with a beautiful voice,
   Which ravish'd you out of your senses;
A pig will make just such a noise
   When his hind leg stuck fast in the fence is.

QUANTITY AND QUALITY

"You can tell about a people from what they eat!" Dr. Sam expounded. "I make this here punch of roasted apples—the English make punch of lemons! You know, undereating sours a people's dispositions, just as overeating dulls 'em, makes them look like they belong in a delicatessen window with an apple in their mouth."

An English visitor to America in 1818 was astounded at the large amount of food available to American farm families. He spent an investigatory year's residence in the United States and found:

As to the manner of living in the country, I was, the other day, at a gentleman's house, and I asked the lady for her bill of fare for the year. I saw fourteen fat hogs, weighing about twenty stone apiece, which were to come into the house the next Monday; for here they slaughter them all in one day. This led me to ask, "Why, in God's name, what do you eat in a year?" The bill of fare was this, for the present year: about this same quantity of hog-meat, four beeves; and forty-six fat sheep! Besides the sucking pigs (of which we had then one on the table), besides lambs, and besides the produce of seventy hen fowls, not to mention good parcels of geese, ducks, and turkeys, but not to forget a garden of three quarters of an acre, and the butter of ten cows, not one ounce of which is ever sold! What do you think of that? Why, you will say, this must be some great overgrown farmer, that has swallowed up half the county; or some nabob sort of merchant. Not at all. He has only 154 acres of land (all he consumes is the produce of this land), and he lives in the same house that his English-born grandfather lived in.

COUNTERPROPAGANDA:
THE WAR OF 1812

Prologue:

> "The Eve of the Battle of Baltimore
> A preacher spoke of peace
> 'The Redcoats,' he said, 'will redden the shore
> For the Lord hath had Surcease!' "

"I addressed 12,000 British on the eve of their expedition to Baltimore. I was afraid when I faced them that their officers, with their keen glittering swords, would cut me in pieces for speaking the truth. But after singing and praying, all fears left me. I told them what kind of a sinner I was and how He had saved me from sin.

". . . I thanked them and the Admiral for their kindness in sparing the camp meeting ground but I could NOT bid them Godspeed in what I understood they were about to do.

"I told them of the great wickedness of war and that God had said: Thou shalt not kill! 'If you do,' I said, 'He will judge you at the last day or before, and he will cause you to perish by the sword!'

"I told them that it was given me from the Almighty that they could not take Baltimore and would not succeed in their expedition.

"We saw them coming back some days later and I went down

to meet the first that landed. 'Have you taken Baltimore?' I asked.

" 'No,' one answered, 'but hundreds of our men have fallen and our best General killed. All the time we were fighting we thought of you and what you told us. You seemed to be standing there before us, still warning us.' "

So you see, The Reverend Joshua Thomas preached peace to the British enemy and, in his way, helped save Baltimore from the British.

AMERICA'S UNCLAIMED UNACCLAIMED
NATIONAL ANTHEM "YANKEE DOODLE":
THE WAR OF 1812

"Yankee Doodle" was given status as America's national anthem only once. It was after the War of 1812. In 1814, Henry Clay and John Quincy Adams were in Ghent ready to sign the treaty of peace between Great Britain and the United States. The citizens of Ghent, on the day of signing, decided to serenade both the British and American Embassies. They knew the British national anthem but not the American, and sent one of the men in the band to ask what it was. Mr. Adams' Negro servant informed him that America's national song was "Yankee Doodle." So the American Embassy was serenaded with a band arrangement of this song. But this was one time only.

Before the War of 1812, when feeling against England was running high again, Americans sang "Yankee Doodle" verses of challenge to Napoleon, who was interfering with our commerce, to Spain, who was still in Florida, and to Great Britain, from whom many wished to take Canada:

> Oh, Yankee Doodle is the tune,
> Americans delight in;
> 'Twill do to whistle, sing or play,
> And just the thing for fighting.

And should Great Britain, Spain or France
Wage war upon our shore, sir;
We'll lead them such a woundy dance
They'll find their toes are sore, sir.

Yankee Doodle boys, Huzza,
Down outside, up the middle;
Yankee Doodle, fa, sol, la,
Trumpet, drum and fiddle!

America's a dandy place
The people are all brothers;
And when one's got a pumpkin pie,
He shares it with the others.

And then on Independence day,
(And who's a better right to?) ;
We eat and drink and sing and play,
And have a dance at night, too.

The land we till is all our own,
Whate'er the price, we paid it!
Therefore we'll fight till all is blue,
Should any dare invade it.

The summary of events, to which the "Yankee Doodle" melody proved so fertile during the American Revolution, found no exception in the War of 1812. After the Battle of New Orleans, an eighteen-stanza popular song, "The New Yankee Doodle," was sung at patriotic gatherings:

Yankee Doodle is the tune,
It comes so nation handy;
And nothing makes a Briton run,
Like Yankee Doodle Dandy!

Come, push about the jorum, boys,
And let us all be merry;
We've had our coffee—now we'll drink,
Our Porter and our Perry.

The wars are o'er and peace is come,
Our foes away are far gone;
We sent the Britons striking home,
And flogged 'em in the bargain.

They thought our sires were dead and gone,
And they could beat us handly;
But soon they found the sons could play,
At Yankee Doodle Dandy!

They first attacked and thought to crush,
Our gallant little Navy;
But Yankee tars soon stopped their grog,
And sent 'em to old Davy!

The foes next tried our boys ashore,
Their Sirs and Lords commanded—
But pretty soon they found themselves,
All Yankee Doodle Dandyed!

Immortal Pike first shipped his troops,
Upon the lake, at Sackett's;
He sought and found the foe at York,
And dusted well their jackets!

The hero there laid down his life,
To raise his country's glory;
As all our sons will pant to do,
Whene'er they hear the story.

Our gallant Pearce then took command,
And stormed the fortress handy;
Our stars were hoisted to the tune,
Of Yankee Doodle Dandy!

There's forty more as brave as they,
But now I can't recall 'em;
Yet long as free men love their rights,
Our country's pride will hail 'em.

The foe at last being tired out,
With many a hearty thrashing;
They all went down to New Orleans,
And thought to get possession.

The troops of Wellington went there,
His brother, too, commanded—
But there again they got themselves,
All Yankee Doodle Dandyed!

The veteran troops who conquered Spain,
Thought that our folks would vanish;
But Jackson settled half their men,
And made the rest talk Spanish.

The foe now thought 'twas time for peace,
And so they made it handy;
For all that they could get from us,
Was Yankee Doodle Dandy!

Then keep the bottle full, my boys
And keep it in rotation;
We'll drink a health to those that fought,
The battles of the nation.

Long may they live, and long enjoy,
The peace they gained so handy;
And teach their sons to play the tune,
Of Yankee Doodle Dandy!

THE HUNTERS OF KENTUCKY

At the Battle of New Orleans, Andrew Jackson and his Kentuckians won out against the British under General Pakenham.

One of the things that made the Kentucky and Tennessee men so formidable during this battle was the Kentucky rifle. James Audubon, the naturalist who was in New Orleans at this time, wrote about the Kentucky rifle:

> That murderous weapon is the means of procuring them subsistence during all their wild and extensive rambles, and is the source of their principal sports and pleasures.

The ballad celebrating the victory of Andrew Jackson was entitled, "The Hunters of Kentucky, or the Battle of New Orleans."

Ye gentlemen and ladies fair
Who grace this famous city
Just listen if you've time to spare,
While I rehearse a ditty:
And for the opportunity
Consider yourselves quite lucky,
For 'tis not often that you see
A hunter from Kentucky.
    O Kentucky, ye hunters of Kentucky!
    O Kentucky, ye hunters of Kentucky!

We are a hardy, free-born race,
Each man to fear a stranger:
What e'er the game we'll join the chase,
Despising time and danger.
And if the daring foe annoys
What e'er his strength and forces,
We'll show him that Kentucky boys
Are alligator horses.
    O Kentucky, ye hunters of Kentucky!
    O Kentucky, ye hunters of Kentucky!

You've heard I s'pose how New Orleans
Is famed for wealth and beauty.
There's girls of every hue it seems
From snowy white to sooty.
So Pakenham he made his brags
If he in fight was lucky,
He'd have their girls and cotton bags,
In spite of old Kentucky.
    O Kentucky, ye hunters of Kentucky!
    O Kentucky, ye hunters of Kentucky!

But Jackson he was wide awake
And was not scar'd at trifles,
For well he knew what aim we take
With our Kentucky rifles.
So he led us down to cypress swamp.
The ground was low and mucky;
There stood John Bull in martial pomp
And here was old Kentucky.
    O Kentucky, ye hunters of Kentucky!
    O Kentucky, ye hunters of Kentucky!

EMIGRATION: SECOND DECADE

The Black Ball Line had an interesting system with European *émigrés* who did not have money. The *émigré* would bind himself to the Captain who would receive the produce of the *émigré's* labor for a certain number of years.

A British passenger to the United States in 1818, Henry B. Feron, wrote a book on a journey through America, entitled *A Narrative of a Journey of 5,000 Miles through America*. He described his voyage and gives us an idea of what emigrants were coming to America, and under what traveling conditions, in the Packet lines:

The passengers on board the brig *Bubona*, from Amsterdam, and who are willing to engage themselves for a limited time, to defray the expenses of their passage, consist of persons of the following occupations, besides women and children, viz.:

13 farmers, 2 bakers, 2 butchers, 8 weavers, 3 taylors, 1 gardener, 3 masons, 1 mill-sawyer, 1 whitesmith, 2 shoemakers, 3 cabinetmakers, 1 coal-burner, 1 barber, 1 carpenter, 1 stocking-weaver, 1 cooper, 1 wheelwright, 1 brewer, 1 locksmith. —Apply on board of the *Bubona*, opposite Callowhill Street, in the river Delaware, or to W. Odlin and Co., No. 38, South Wharves, Oct. 2.

As we ascended the side of this hulk, a most revolting scene of want and misery presented itself. The eye involuntarily turned for some relief from the horrible picture of human suffering, which this living sepulchre afforded. Mr. _____ enquired if there were any shoe-makers on board. The captain advanced; his appearance bespoke his office; he is an American, tall, determined, and with an eye that flashes with Algerine cruelty. He called in the Dutch language for shoe-makers, and never can I forget the scene which followed. The poor fellows came running up with unspeakable delight, no doubt anticipating a relief from their loathsome dungeon. Their clothes, if rags deserve that denomination, actually perfumed the air. Some were without shirts, others had this article of dress, but of a quality as coarse as the worst packing cloth. I enquired of several if they could speak English. They smiled and gabbed, "No Engly, no Engly,—one Engly talk ship." The deck was filthy. The cooking, washing, and necessary departments were close together. Such is the mercenary barbarity of the Americans who are engaged in this trade, that they crammed into one of those vessels 500 passengers, 80 of whom died on the passage. The price for women is about 70 dollars, men 80 dollars, boys 60 dollars.

The steerage passengers had a bad time of it, both as to accommodations and food. Their staple meal was oatmeal and water boiled into a mush. They did their own cooking in that part of the ship that was open to the weather, in pots slung from hooks on a rail over the fires. On the larger ships women often waited hours for their turn. In bad weather no cooking was possible. Ports were sealed tight, hatches were battened down. It was no unusual thing for death and epidemics to rage before the end of a voyage. On those boats where food rations were doled out once a week, they consisted in the beginning of rice, salt pork, and hard tack. By later regulations, an additional ration of bread and potatoes were demanded. Depending on the boat, there was often a variation in the amount of water or the amount of molasses that supplemented this diet.

The classes of food and accommodations were paralleled by the classes of passengers. The first-class passenger lived in trim, comfortable cabins aft. For the first-class passengers food was carried alive. For fresh milk there was a cow shed; for fresh eggs there were hens roosting in the long boats; pigs, ducks, and geese were penned near the galley on the ships. The crew lived forward in forecastle and the steerage passengers lived between decks. On most ships, the arrangement about food was that the sailors had a steady diet of hard tack and salt beef.

Dr. Sam had sailed the Atlantic under thirty thousand square feet of canvas, seen many kinds of women and seaports, yet as he drew nearer the autumn of his days, he grew fonder of America and the girls he saw along the banks. "A man's heart sails best," he said aptly, as he maneuvred a flat-bottomed boat carrying me and a young lady down the Ambrose River, "when summer's turning to fall, on a day like this when there's just breeze enough to fill sixteen square feet of a young lady's gingham."

DRUNKENNESS

September 3, 1818. To-day I have seen a man sprawling on the ground in a state of intoxication; he is a native of Ireland. This is the first instance of the kind which I have seen in America. From this incident, I do not mean to represent that the people here do not drink spiritous liquors. The truth is, that many drink of them almost the moment after they get out of bed, and also at frequent intervals during the day; but though this fact has been noticed, the first conclusion is nevertheless true, that excessive drinking is rare.   James Flint, *Letters from America*

Dr. Sam waxed wrathful. "I know the truth of this tale, from my Uncle Sam, and a story half-told is a story untold! That Irish lad got up, joined the Boston Fire Brigade where he drank gin and molasses with his fellow countrymen and ever after sang the virtues of sorghum!" He let go his lusty Harvard tenor:

> But oh! Let sorghum's sable god deplore
> Those engine-heroes so reknown of yore!

"My Uncle Sam put him onto sorghum," the doctor reminisced. "Jest like your Mammy used to physic you with in the

springtime . . . except without the sulphur! Fire precautions!"
He took a little corn for his health's sake. "Bless you, lad, this is the sweetest drink that ever streaked down a man's gullet."

62

RED JACKET AND CHRISTIANITY

The Senecas were the most important tribe of the Six Nations, and their most famous chief was called Red Jacket by the whites. He was noted for his noble and dignified behavior, although it is said that in later years he was addicted to the use of "ardent spirits."

Many of his tribe became Christians, but Red Jacket refused to be converted. It is interesting that he would not become a Christian because he could not understand how the Indians had any participation in the guilt of the Crucifixion. To a clergyman who was importuning him on the subject, Red Jacket said:

Brother, as your white men murdered the Son of the Great Spirit we Indians had nothing to do with it, and it is none of our affair. If He had come among us, we would not have killed Him; we would have treated Him well. You must make amends for that crime yourselves.

He also said:

Brother, you say there is but one way to worship and serve the Great Spirit; if there is but one religion, why do white people differ so much about it? Why not agree, as you can read the same book. . . . If this book was intended for us as well as you, why has not the Great Spirit given it to us and not only to us, why did He not give to our forefathers the knowledge of that book with the means of understanding it rightly? We only know what you tell us about it; how shall we know when to believe, being so often deceived by the white people?. . . . We are told that your religion was given to your forefathers and has been handed down from father to son. We also have a religion which was given to our forefathers and has been handed down to us their children. We worship that way. It teacheth us to be thankful for all the favors we receive; to love each other and to be united; we never quarrel about religion. . . . Brother, the Great Spirit has made us all; but He has made a great difference between his white and red children. Since He has made so great a difference between us in other things, why may we not conclude that He has given us a different religion according to our understanding; the Great Spirit does right; He knows what is best for His children; we are satisfied. Brother, we do not wish to disappoint your religion or take it from you; we only want to enjoy our own.

THE AMERICAN LANGUAGE

All visitors to America in the nineteenth century seem to
have been amazed at the language they found. This was especially true of English visitors to whom American colloquialisms
sounded a strange note. Charles Dickens, for example, was surprised to find an extensive use of the word "fix." Here is what
he had to say about it:

There are few words which perform such various duties as
this word "fix." It is the Caleb Quotem of the American
vocabulary. You call upon a gentleman in a country town,
and his help informs you that he is "fixing himself" just
now, but will be down directly: by which you are to understand that he is dressing. You inquire, on board a steamboat, of a fellow-passenger, whether breakfast will be ready
soon, and he tells you he should think so, for when he was
last below, they were "fixing the tables": in other words,
laying the cloth. You beg a porter to collect your luggage,
and he entreats you not to be uneasy, for he'll "fix it presently": and if you complain of indisposition, you are advised to have recourse to Doctor So-and-so, who will "fix
you" in no time.

One night, I ordered a bottle of mulled wine at an hotel
where I was staying, and waited a long time for it; at length
it was put upon the table with an apology from the land-

lord that he feared it wasn't "fixed properly." And I recollect once, at a stage-coach dinner, overhearing a very stern gentleman demand of a waiter who presented him with a plate of underdone roast-beef, whether he called that, "fixing God A'mighty's vittles?"

WHO READS AN AMERICAN BOOK: 1820

By 1820, most of the United States had a very definite attitude toward Europe, and Europe had a very definite attitude toward the United States.

Europe was curious and interested in the roughness and pioneering of the new country, and all over the new country there was a great contempt for the decadence of Europe. Perhaps this was due to the fact that the Europeans who swarmed into America were for the most part the poor and disinherited of the Continent. It is true that in the eastern cities, where learning and culture had a high premium, there was embarrassment before the cultural reaches of Europe. Even though it was felt that our universities were on a par with the European universities, it was also felt that America offered no background. This feeling was only intensified when Sydney Smith wrote a criticism in the *Edinburgh Review* that read this way:

In the four quarters of the globe, who reads an American book, or goes to an American play, or looks at an American picture or statue? What does the world yet owe to American physicians or surgeons? What new substances have their chemists discovered, or what old ones have they analysed? What new constellations have been discovered by the telescopes of Americans?—What have they done in the mathematics? Who drinks out of American glasses? or eats from American plates? or wears American coats or gowns? or sleeps in American blankets?—Finally, under which of the old tyrannical governments of Europe is every sixth man a Slave, whom his fellow creatures may buy and sell and torture?

It seems we have improved some. . . . However, some Europeans still agree with Mr. Smith in spirit.

65

MARRIAGE AND MISTRESSES

Dr. Sam never did think much of the matrimonial state, and as evidence of woman's deceitfulness would carefully unfold a tattered bit of letter from his billfold. It was, he assured me, a letter written by his aunt to his mother.

It looked very sedate to me until he suggested I read each *alternate* line:

> I cannot be satisfied, my dearest friend!
> blest as I am in the matrimonial state,
> unless I pour into your friendly bosom,
> which has ever been in unison with mine,
> the various sensations which swell
> with the liveliest emotion of pleasure,
> my almost bursting heart. I tell you my dear
> husband is the most amiable of men,
> I have now been married seven weeks, and
> never have found the least reason to
> repent the day that joined us. My husband is
> both in person and manners far from resembling
> ugly, cross, old, disagreeable, and jealous
> monsters, who think by confining to secure—
> a wife, it is his maxim to treat as a
> bosom friend and confidant, and not as a
> plaything, or menial slave, the woman

chosen to be his companion. Neither party
he says, should always obey implicitly;
but each yield to the other by turns.
An ancient maiden aunt, near seventy,
a cheerful, venerable, and pleasant old lady,
lives in the house with us; she is the delight of both young and old; she is civil to all the neighborhood round,
generous and charitable to the poor.
I am convinced my husband loves nothing more
than he does me; he flatters me more
than a glass; and his intoxication
(for so I must call the excess of his love)
often makes me blush for the unworthiness
of its object, and wish I could be more deserving
of the man whose name I bear. To
say all in one word, my dear, and to
crown the whole—my former gallant lover
is now my indulgent husband; my husband
is returned, and I might have had
a prince without the felicity I find in
him. Adieu! may you be blest as I am unable to wish that I could be more
happy.

"*Tot homines, quot sententiae!* That's Latin, Son! It means
each man gets his own kind of life sentence!" Dr. Sam winked
sagely. "And mine is observation! Who marries for love takes
a wife; who marries for convenience takes a mistress; who marries from consideration takes a lady. You are loved by your
wife, regarded by your mistress, tolerated by your lady. You
have a wife for yourself, a mistress for your house and its
friends, a lady for the world. Your wife will agree with you,
your mistress will accommodate you, your lady will manage
you. Your wife will take care of your household, your mistress
of your house, your lady of appearances. If you are sick, your

wife will nurse you, your mistress will visit you, your lady will inquire after your health. You take a walk with your wife, a ride with your mistress, and join parties with your lady. Your wife will share your grief, your mistress your money, and your lady your debts. If you are dead, your wife will shed tears, your mistress lament, and your lady wear mourning. Be guided by this!"

66

SLAVERY IN AMERICA

I

In the early nineteenth century, Negro slavery was recognized as a fact in America, and seldom considered a problem. However, James Flint, the Englishman, from whose country slavery had been abolished some time back, includes in his book a conversation with a Negro reaping wheat on a Long Island farm in 1818:

> I went into a field where a Negro was reaping wheat . . . and observed that about an English acre was cut down. On making inquiry, it appeared that he had been engaged about six hours in the work. The following dialogue ensued:
> "You work very hard?"
> "No Sir, I can do much more in the time, but that of no use."
> "You are not free then?"
> "No Sir, I a slave, I 'longs to Jacob Van _____, there," (pointing to the farm house.)
> "But you black people are very well treated here?"
> "Oh yes, Sir, master very good to me, give me everything to eat he eat self, but no Sunday clothes."
> "You may live happier than some poor free people?"

"That may be true, Sir, but put bird in cage, give him plenty to eat, still he fly away."

II

Another and earlier English traveler in America, James Melish, gives this description of the execution of a Savannah Negro who had killed an overseer:

Leaving Hely's Inn, near Savannah, we travelled two miles, when my fellow-traveller stopped to point out the spot where two Negroes were executed for killing an overseer. The one was hanged and the other burnt to death. I was informed that this mode of punishment is sometimes inflicted on Negroes, when the crime is very flagrant, to deprive them of the mental consolation arising from a hope that they will after death return to their own country. This may be good policy as respects the blacks; but, in mercy to the white people, I wish it could be avoided. When I looked at the scorched tree where the man had been tied, and observed the fragments of his bones at the foot of it, I was horror-struck; and I never yet can think of the scene without a pang. What feelings must have been excited in those who saw the execution!

A SLAVE AUCTION

A later traveler in America, Captain Basil Hall, found himself at a slave auction in Washington, and his account of the proceedings reveals the struggle that sometimes ensued between sentiment and the practical aspects of slave trading:

After various delays, the slave was put up at auction, at the end of the passage, near which four or five persons had by this time collected. There was a good deal of laughing and talking amongst the buyers, and several jests were sported on the occasion, of which their little victim took no more notice than if he had been a horse or a dog. In fact, he was not a chubby shining little negro, with a flat nose, thick lips, and woolly hair, but a slender, delicate-looking youth, more yellow than black, with an expression every way suitable, I thought, with the forlorn situation in which he was placed—for both his parents, and all his brothers and sisters, he told me, had been long ago sold into slavery, and sent to the Southern States, Florida or Alabama, he knew not where!

"Well, gentlemen," cried the Deputy-Marshall, "will you give us a bid? Look at him—as smart a fellow as ever you saw—works like a tiger!"

One of the spectators called out, "Come, I'll say 25 dollars"—another said 35—another said 40—and at last 100 dollars were bid for him.

From the spot where I was standing in the corner, behind the rest of the party, I could see all that was passing. I felt my pulse accelerating at each successive offer, and my cheek getting flushed—for the scene was so very new that I almost fancied I was dreaming.

The interest, after a time, took a different character, to which, however, I by no means wished to give utterance, or in any shape to betray; but at this moment the Deputy-Marshal, finding the price to hang at 100 dollars, looked over to me and said, "Do give us a bid, sir—won't you?"

My indignation was just beginning to boil over at this juncture, and I cried out, in answer to this appeal, with more asperity than good sense or good breeding—"No! No! I thank God we don't do such things in my country!"

"And I wish, with all my heart," said the auctioneer, in a tone that made me sorry for having spoken so hastily, "I wish we did not do such things here."

"Amen!" said several voices.

The sale went on.

OLD GRIMES
By Albert G. Greene. 1827

Old Grimes is dead—that good old man—
  We ne'er shall see him more;
He wore a single-breasted coat
  That buttoned down before.

His heart was open as the day,
  His feelings all were true;
His hair was some inclined to gray,
  He wore it in a queue.

Whene'er was heard the voice of pain,
  His breast with pity burned;
The large round head upon his cane
  From ivory was turned.

Thus ever prompt at pity's call,
  He knew no base design;
His eyes were dark, and rather small,
  His nose was aquiline.

He lived at peace with all mankind,
  In friendship he was true;
His coat had pocket holes behind,
  His pantaloons were blue.

But poor old Grimes is now at rest,
  Nor fears misfortune's frown;
He had a double-breasted vest,
  The stripes ran up and down.

He modest merit sought to find,
  And pay it its desert;

He had no malice in his mind,
  No ruffle on his shirt.

His neighbors he did not abuse;
  Was sociable and gay;
He wore not rights and lefts for shoes,
  But changed them every day.

His knowledge, hid from public gaze,
  He never brought to view;
Nor made a noise town-meeting days,
  As many people do.

Thus undisturbed by anxious cares,
  His peaceful moments ran;
And every body said he was
  A fine old gentleman.

AMERICA'S UNCLAIMED UNACCLAIMED
NATIONAL ANTHEM: YANKEE DOODLE:
FROM LOVE TO POLITICS
(PRE-CIVIL WAR)

One of the most widely-read English travelers to the United States was Mrs. Frances Trollope. She found little to admire in the manners and customs she found here and her work was much resented. She wrote an ill-tempered book, *The Domestic Manners of the Americans,* which was published in London in 1832 and sold at a great rate. The more the book was abused, the more rapidly new editions appeared. According to Mrs. Trollope, the Americans were ill-mannered, crude, money-grabbing and boastful. What is more, she wrote, they all sang a very bad tune called "Yankee Doodle":

Once in Ohio, and once in the District of Columbia, I had an atlas displayed before me, that I might be convinced by the evidence of my own eyes what a very contemptible little country I came from. I shall never forget the gravity with which, on the latter occasion, a gentleman . . . showed me, past contradiction, that the whole of the British dominions did not equal in size one of their least important states; nor the air with which, after the demonstration, he placed his feet upon the chimney-piece, considerably higher than his head, and whistled Yankee Doodle.

The 1830's and 1840's saw the development of individual and family group performers. The minstrel show became an accepted and popular theatrical form. "Yankee Doodle" found a place on the stage. Believe it or not, there was a love ballad about a soldier and his peerless maid to the "Yankee Doodle" melody:

> A soldier wooed a peerless maid,
> Soft love his bosom swelling,
> And as they on the mountain strayed,
> His tender tale was telling.
>
> When across the distant vale,
> They heard the war drums rattle,
> The trumpets sounding in the gale,
> Called him from love to battle.
>
> The soldier looked a long adieu,
> His breast with ardor growing,
> And she with sobs sad, soft, and true,
> Beheld her lover going.
>
> "Fare thee well," the soldier cried,
> "Again the war drums rattle."
> A fervent prayer to heaven she sighed,
> To bring him back from battle.
>
> The soldier fell among the slain,
> Upon the bed of glory;
> And, from another favored swain,
> She heard the fatal story.
>
> "I thought," said she, " 'twould be his last,
> When I heard the war drums rattle;
> Had he stayed here he'd not been shot,
> So never go to battle."

The 1820's, '30's, and '40's saw the construction of railroads, the development of the steamboat, the ascension of the first balloon, the development of the electric telegraph and the craze over "magnetism" (another word for hypnotism). The tee-totalers had a temperance society and the American national debt was causing great concern. The nation became acquainted with these factors in another "Yankee Doodle" song:

> O, the world ain't now as it used to was,
> The past is like a dream, sirs;
> Ev'rything's on the railroad plan,
> Though they don't all go by steam, sirs.

> Expresses now are all the rage,
> By steamboat and balloon, sirs;
> In a year or two we'll get the news,
> Directly from the moon, sirs.

> The 'lectric telegraphs are new,
> Both time and distance mocking;
> But then, the news that they convey,
> Is really very shocking.

> A pint of water, an ounce of chalk,
> Together mix'd make cream, sirs;
> The hens have only to lay their eggs,
> And the chickens are hatch'd by steam, sir.

> Should you wish to kiss a girl,
> And not at all surprise her;
> The method's as simple as A, B, C,
> You first must "magnetize" her.

> They've prov'd that laughter's a lightsome thing,
> In ev'ry lad and lass, sirs;

For when you want to snigger out,
Just swallow laughing-gas, sirs.

Consistency is well enough,
In every little matter;
But the "totalers" with a drop of gin,
Sometimes dilute their water.

Crime is not now what once it was,
In England, France or Spain, sirs;
If a man takes a notion to cut your throat,
It's just that he's insane, sirs!

If demagogues, too deep in debt,
Should chance to sink the nation;
Why the proper way to cancel it,
Is by repudiation!

In 1836, Texas fought for and won its independence from Mexico. In 1846, America fought Mexico in order to preserve the independence of Texas. Annexation was in the minds of many, even then. At the same time the United States, led by President Polk, was in controversy with England over the Territory of Oregon. Many thought that England was secretly inciting the Mexicans to fight in order to draw American troops and interest from the Oregon border. Uncle Sam's song to Miss Texas:

> (Chorus)
> Yankee Doodle is the word,
> Surpassing all creation,
> With the pipe or with the sword,
> It makes us love our nation.

Walk in my tall-haired Indian gal,
Your hand, my star-eyed Texas;

You're welcome to our White House Hall,
Tho 'Mexy's hounds would vex us;
Come on and take some Johnny-cake,
With 'lasses snug and coodle,
For that and independence make
A full-blood Yankee Doodle.

My overseer, young Jimmy Polk,
Shall show you all my nieces;
And then the cabinet we'll smoke,
Until our eagle sneezes;
If Johnny Bull's fat greedy boys,
About our Union grumble,
I'll kick up sich a tarnal noise,
'Twill make 'em feel quite humble.

If Mexy, backed by secret foes,
Still talks of taking you, gal,
Why, we can lick 'em all, you know,
An' then annex 'em too, gal;
For freedom's great millenium,
Is working earth's salvation,
Her sassy kingdom soon will come,
Annexin' all creation.

And so we fought the Mexican War. Did the soldiers fight
for liberty and freedom? Well, here's their "Yankee Doodle"
song, "We're the Boys from Mexico":

We're the boys from Mexico,
Sing Yankee Doodle Dandy,
Gold and Silver images,
Plentiful and handy.

The Mexicans are doomed to fall,
God has in wrath forsook 'em,

And all their goods and chattels call
On us to go and hook 'em.

Churches grand, with altars rich,
Saints with diamond collars,
(That's the talk to understand)
With lots of bright new dollars.

The Mexicans have cut up high,
And we have let 'em do it,
Till they have got our "dander riz"
And now they'll have to rue it.

We have a corps of editors,
Each with a mighty bellows,
To strike a mortal terror in
Them tarnal Spanish fellows.

And when we've laid aside our arms,
With nothing more to vex us,
We'll vote ourselves extensive farms,
Each one as big as Texas.

And when our flag has been upheld,
And crushed lies each presumer,
We'll open "free and easy's" in
The Halls of Montezumer.

James K. Polk had been elected on a platform calling for the annexation of Texas and "Fifty-four-Forty or Fight" on the Oregon question. The campaign that elected Polk against Henry Clay was probably one of the most musical in our history. First the Clay adherents brought out a little book of songs written to well-known melodies, called *The Clay Minstrel*. The theme song of the book was "Yankee Doodle" and it went like this:

Shout Yankee Doodle! Whigs, Huzza!
We're done with Captain Tyler;

223

He who has been his country's flaw,
Shall never more defile 'er.

For Farmer Clay then boys hurrah—
And proudly here proclaim him:
The great, the good, the valiant Hal,
And shout whene'er you name him!

For long and loud the country calls,
For the bold Ashland farmer;
Bravest when danger most appalls;
With him, no foe shall harm 'er.

Brave Whigs, whene'er the gallant song,
"Log cabins and hard cider,"
Was chorused loud and echo'd long,
Let this be heard—and wider!

Polk adherents were not to be outdone and immediately put out their own songbook entitled *Democratic Lute and Folk and Dallas Minstrel*. They, too, had a "Yankee Doodle" theme song:

With Polk and Dallas in our van,
Say, what have we to fear, sirs?
Poor Henry Clay's a used-up name,
His party's in the rear, sirs.

The people will have better men,
To execute their laws, sirs;
The magic names of Tip and Ty,
To humbug folks won't do, sirs.

Their coons are dead, their cabins down,
Hard cider grown quite stale, sirs;

And at the people's with'ring frown,
Their leader grows quite pale, sirs.

Even Abraham Lincoln was elected to a "Yankee Doodle"
campaign song:

Yankee Doodle does as well,
As anybody can, sir;
And like the ladies, he's for Abe,
And Union to a man, sir.

Yankee Doodle never fails,
When he resolves to try, sir;
To elect a man who can't split rails,
That's just "all my eye, sir."

Yankee Doodle's come to town,
And on mature reflection;
He's gonna do the slavites brown,
At the next election.

Yankee Doodle cuts a swell,
Although he will not bet, sir;
Yet he goes in for Abraham,
And Hamlin of old Maine, sir.

And so that our little campaign for the recognition of "Yankee Doodle" as a unique, ever-useful, everlasting known melody
may once again show its usefulness, how about this courting
ballad?

My daddy to my mammy said,
"Do marry me, my dear miss."
My mammy, blushing, hung her head
And softly sighed, "Oh yes!"

My daddy loved his backer pipe,
My mother loved her poodle,
Till I appeared a cherry ripe,
Dear little Yankee Doodle.

My beauty was so great and grand,
To kiss me each would squeeze;
My mouth was like a haystack,
And my lips like buttered peas.

When breeched, at length, ye gods! how fine!
'Tis true or I'm a noodle,
They called me then the genuine
Right charming Yankee Doodle.

The most correctest possibly
Of hofficers I am;
Lauks, how the gals all laughs at I,
And how I laughs at 'em!

But 'tis my beauty makes of all
The most completest noodle,
They loves me long, short, large and small,
The dashing Yankee Doodle.

A captain millinary deck't,
Take heed, ye lovely friskers,
For very soon I does expect
To vear a pair of viskers.

But with a tear I now departs,
Don't think vot I'm a noodle;
If I stays here you'll lose your hearts,
Aye, all to Yankee Doodle.

THE PLIGHT OF THE INDIAN: 1831

Alexis de Tocqueville spent nine months of 1830 visiting
the principal cities of America, going out to the frontier and
Indian settlements. Everywhere, he questioned, listened, and
analyzed, and then wrote one of the most penetrating studies of
this country at the time. He called his book *Democracy in
America*. In certain pertinent paragraphs, he went to the heart
of the condition of "the American aborigine":

When the Indians were the sole inhabitants of the wilds
from whence they have since been expelled, their wants
were few. Their arms were of their own manufacture, their
only drink was the water of the brook, and their clothes
consisted of the skins of animals, whose flesh furnished
them with food.

The Europeans introduced among the savages of North
America firearms, ardent spirits, and iron; they taught
them to exchange for manufactured stuffs the rough garments which had previously satisfied their untutored sim-
plicity. Having acquired new tastes, without the arts by
which they could be gratified, the Indians were obliged to
have recourse to the workmanship of the Whites; but in
return for their productions the savage had nothing to
offer except the rich furs which still abounded in his woods.
Hence the chase became necessary, not merely to provide

for his subsistence, but in order to procure the only objects of barter which he could furnish to Europe. While the wants of the natives were thus increasing, their resources continued to diminish.

From the moment when a European settlement is formed in the neighborhood of the territory occupied by the Indians, the beasts of chase take the alarm. Thousands of savages, wandering the forests and destitute of any fixed dwelling, did not disturb them; but as soon as the continuous sounds of European labour are heard in their neighbourhood, they begin to flee away, and retire to the West, where their instinct teaches them that they will find deserts of immeasurable extent. . . .

To drive away their game is to deprive the Indians of the means of existence as effectually as if the fields of our agriculturists were stricken with barrenness; and they are reduced, like famished wolves, to prowl through the forsaken woods in quest of prey. Their instinctive love of their country attaches them to the soil which gave them birth, even after it has ceased to yield anything but misery and death. At length they are compelled to acquiesce, and to depart: they follow the traces of the elk, the buffalo, and the beaver, and are guided by these wild animals in the choice of their future country. Properly speaking, therefore, it is not the Europeans who drive away the native inhabitants of America; it is famine which compels them to recede; a happy distinction which had escaped the casuists of former times, and for which we are indebted to modern discovery!

It is impossible to conceive the extent of the sufferings which attend these forced emigrations. They are undertaken by a people already exhausted and reduced; and the countries to which the newcomers betake themselves are inhabited by other tribes which receive them with jealous hostility. Hunger is in the rear; war awaits them, and misery besets them on all sides. In the hope of escaping

from such a host of enemies, they separate, and each individual endeavours to procure the means of supporting
his existence in solitude and secrecy, living in the im-
mensity of the desert like an outcast in civilized society.
The social tie, which distress had long since weakened, is
then dissolved; they have lost their country, and their
people soon desert them: their very families are obliter-
ated; the names they bore in common are forgotten, their
language perishes, and all traces of their origin disappear.
Their nation has ceased to exist, except in the recollection
of the antiquaries of America and a few of the learned
of Europe. . . .

71

INDIAN TO THE WEST

We can think of the American Indian just as we can think of the displaced persons of our own time. *The New York Observer* of 1839 carried this account of a group of Cherokee Indians dispossessed of their lands and forced to move westward:

The last detachment which we passed on the 7th embraced rising two thousand Indians with horses and mules in proportion. The forward part of the train we found just pitching their tents for the night, and notwithstanding some thirty or forty wagons were already stationed, we found the road literally filled with the procession for about three miles in length. The sick and feeble were carried in wagons—about as comfortable for travelling as a New England ox cart with a covering over it—a great many ride on horseback and multitudes go on foot—even aged females, apparently nearly ready to drop into the grave, were travelling with heavy burdens attached to the back—on the sometimes frozen ground, and sometimes muddy streets, with no covering for the feet except what nature had given them. We were some hours making our way through the crowd, which brought us in close contact with the wagons and multitude, so much that we felt fortunate to find ourselves freed from the crowd without leaving any part of our carriage. We learned from the inhabitants on the road where the Indians passed, that they buried fourteen or fifteen at every stopping place, and they make a journey of ten miles per day only on an average. One fact which to my own mind seemed a lesson indeed to the American nation is, that they will not travel on the Sabbath . . . when the Sabbath came, they must stop, and not merely stop—they must worship the Great Spirit, too, for they had divine service on the Sabbath—a camp-meeting in truth.

HOW THE CHRISTMAS TREE
CAME TO THE UNITED STATES

Harriet Martineau, English visitor to the United States, spent Christmas, 1835, in Boston. She visited at the household of a family whose child, Charley, made great claim to her affection. The German Christmas tree was not known to this country at the time:

I was present at the introduction into the new country of the German Christmas-tree. My little friend Charley and three companions had been long preparing for this pretty show. The cook had broken her eggs carefully in the middle for some weeks past, that Charley might have the shells for cups; and these cups were gilded and coloured very prettily. I rather think it was, generally speaking, a secret out of the house; but I knew what to expect. . . . It was desirable that our preparations should be completed before the little folks should begin to arrive; and we were all engaged in sticking on the last of the seven dozen of wax-tapers, and in filling the gilded egg-cups and gay paper cornucopiae with comfits, lozenges, and barley-sugar. The tree was the top of a young fir, planted in a tub, which was ornamented with moss. Smart dolls and other whimsies glittered in the evergreen, and there was not a twig

which had not something sparkling upon it. When the
sound of wheels was heard, we had just finished; and we
shut up the tree by itself in the front drawing-room, while
we went into the other, trying to look as if nothing was
going to happen. Charley looked a good deal like himself,
only now and then twisting himself about in an unaccount-
able fit of giggling. It was a very large party; for, besides
the tribes of children, there were papas and mammas,
uncles, aunts and elder sisters. When all were come we
shut out the cold; the great fire burned clearly; the tea and
coffee were as hot as possible, and the cheeks of the little
ones grew rosier and their eyes brighter every moment.
It had been settled that, in order to cover our designs, I
was to resume my vocation of teaching Christmas games
after tea, while Charley's mother and her maids went to
light up the front room. So all found seats, many of the
children on the floor, for Old Coach. . . . When they were
fairly practised in the game, I turned over my story to a
neighbour, and got away to help to light up the tree. . . .

I mounted the steps behind the tree to see the effect of
opening the doors. It was delightful. The children poured
in, but in a moment every voice was hushed. Their faces
were upturned to the blaze, all eyes wide open, all lips
parted, all steps arrested. Nobody spoke, only Charley
leaped for joy. The first symptom of recovery was the
children's wandering round the tree. At last a quick pair
of eyes discovered that it bore something eatable, and from
that moment the babble began again. They were told that
they might get what they could without burning themselves; and we tall people kept watch, and helped them
with good things from the higher branches. When all had
had enough, we returned to the larger room, and finished
the evening with dancing. By ten o'clock all were well
warmed for the ride home with steaming mulled wine, and
the prosperous evening closed with shouts of mirth. By a
little after eleven Charley's father and mother and I were

left by ourselves to sit in the new year. I have little doubt the Christmas-tree will become one of the most flourishing exotics of New England. . . .

73

TRAVEL GUIDE: 1837

Every seaboard town had its guidebook to the West, published for the benefit of newcomers and those who were anxious to move on. One of the most famous was *Peck's New Guide to the West*, published in Boston in 1837, and containing this description of the progression of all western settlements:

First comes the pioneer who depends for subsistence . . . upon the natural growth of vegetation and the proceeds of hunting . . . his efforts are directed mainly to a crop of corn and a "truck patch." He builds his cabin, gathers around him a few families of similar taste . . . till the neighbors crowd around and he lacks elbow room. He disposes of cabin and corn field to the next class of emigrants and "breaks for the high timber". . . .

The next class of emigrants purchase the lands . . . and exhibit the picture and forms of plain, frugal, civilized life . . . The men of capital and enterprise come. The settler is ready to sell out . . . push farther into the interior and become himself a man of capital and enterprise . . .

BUCK AND GAG

The volunteer army of the Mexican War was a rough and motley aggregation, hard-fighting, but totally undisciplined. Many of the officers were but little better than the men. Murders, near-mutinies, and even desertion to the enemy were not unknown. Consequently, punishments were severe. Hangings were rather frequent and lacking in finesse. On several occasions the prisoner, with a rope about his neck, was placed in a wagon and driven under the gallows. The end of the rope was fastened to the crossbeam, the wagon was driven away, and the poor devil was left dangling.

A common punishment was "bucking and gagging." The victim was placed on his back on the ground. His outspread arms and legs were tied to stakes, and a gag was placed in his mouth.

> Come, all Yankee soldiers, give ear to my song.
> It is a short ditty, it will not keep you long;
> It is of no use to fret, on account of our luck,
> We can laugh, drink, and sing yet, in spite of the buck.
>
> "Sergeant, buck and gag him," our officers cry,
> For each trifling offense which they happen to spy,
> Till with bucking and gagging of Dick, Tom, Pat
>   and Bill,
> Faith, the Mexican's ranks they have helped to fill.

The treatment they give us, as all of us know,
Is bucking and gagging for whipping the foe;
They buck and gag us for malice or spite,
But they are glad to release us when going to fight.

A poor soldier tied up in the hot sun or rain,
With a gag in his mouth till he's tortured with pain,
Why, I'm blessed if the eagle, we wear on our flag,
In its claws couldn't carry a buck and a gag.

AUTOGRAPHS

"Mobbing a man for his autograph, implies a great lack of respect," Dr. Sam aired himself thus, in his matter-of-fact way. "Yet all that standing in line and walking of miles and waiting for the quarry carries a rough-hewn veneration! Therefore I counsel the giving of autographs! Why, if ever one of these fellers who says he is a Messiah, really is . . . they'd get Him, and that'd make mighty handy testimony!" He began his finishing run and the quirk of humor in his eye made his irreverence worthy of a reverent hearing. ". . . but you ain't one of them! Therefore, sign your autographs with a crowquill, for name droppings, like bird droppings, bring blessings upon the heads of the taker and the giver."

It has been thought by us that an incessant request for autographs is peculiar to our times. Obviously, this is not so, for Harriet Martineau found in Washington, D.C., during the terms of Andrew Jackson, that autograph seekers were constantly present:

When I was at Washington, albums were the fashion and the plague of the day. I scarcely ever came home but I found an album on my table or requests for autographs; but some ladies went much further than petitioning a foreigner who might be supposed to have leisure. I have actually seen them stand at the door of the Senate Chamber, and send the doorkeeper with an album, and a request to write in it, to Mr. Webster and other eminent members. I have seen them do worse; stand at the door of the Supreme Court, and send in their albums to Chief-Justice Marshall while he was on the bench hearing pleadings. The poor president was terribly persecuted; and to him it was a real nuisance, as he had no poetical resource but Watt's hymns. I have seen verses and stanzas of a most ominous purport from Watts, in the president's very conspicuous handwriting, standing in the midst of the crowquill compliments and translucent charades which are the staple of albums. Nothing was done to repress this atrocious impertinence of the ladies. I always declined writing more than name and date; but senators, judges, and statesmen submitted to write gallant nonsense at the request of any woman who would stoop to desire it. . . .

76

BALLROOM DANCING

Dances were accepted events in every city, ranging all the way from the staid formal balls of the "socialites" to the rowdy waterfront dances of the keel-boat men and tavern brawlers. There is an interesting description of a St. Louis ball given by one of the many traveling Englishmen, Charles Augustus Murray. He was shocked by the violence of many of the Mississippi River towns but equally moved by the primness of St. Louis dancing:

> No imagination can conceive the rolling, the swinging, the strange undulations of the rotary pair. They frequently hold each other only by one hand, and the lady places her idle hand on her waist; while the gentleman flourishes his gracefully either above his own or his partner's head, or assigns to it some resting-place no less extraordinary than its movements. In some circles in the South, elbow-waltzing alone is permitted; the lady's waist is forbidden ground, and the gentleman is compelled to hold her by the points of the elbows.

A quite different description is given of a public ball held in a frame building in Chicago, at a time when that city was still considered a trading post. This time an American traveler, a Mr. Charles F. Hoffman, was invited to the dance and ushered into:

. . . . a tolerably sized dancing room, occupying the second story of the house, and having its unfinished walls so ingeniously covered with pine-branches and flags borrowed from the garrison, that, with the white-washed ceiling above, it presented a very complete and quite pretty appearance. It was not so warm, however, that the fires of cheerful hickory, which roared at either end, could have been readily dispensed with. An orchestra of unplaned boards was raised against the wall in the center of the room; the band consisting of a dandy negro with his violin, a fine military-looking bass drummer from the fort, and a volunteer citizen, who alternately played an accompaniment upon the flute and triangle. Blackie, who flourished about with a great many airs and graces, was decidedly the king of the company, and it was amusing, while his head followed the direction of his fiddle-bow with pertinacious fidelity, to see the Captain Manual-like precision with which the soldier dressed to the front on one side, and the nonchalant air of importance which the citizen attempted to preserve on the other.

As for the company, it was such a complete medley of all ranks, ages, professions, trades, and occupations, brought together from all parts of the world, and now for the first time brought together, that it was amazing to witness the decorum with which they commingled on this festive occasion. The managers (among whom were some officers of the garrison) must certainly be au fait at dressing a lobster and mixing regent's punch, in order to have produced a harmonious compound from such a collection of contrarieties. The gayest figure that was ever called by quadrille playing Benoit never afforded me half the amusement that did these Chicago cotillions. Here you might see a veteran officer in full uniform balancing to a tradesman's daughter still in her short frock and trousers, while there the golden aiguillette of a handsome surgeon flapped in unison with the glass beads upon a scrawny neck of fifty. In one

241

quarter, the high-placed buttons of a linsey-woolsey coat would be dos-a-dos to the elegantly turned shoulders of a delicate-looking southern girl; and in another, a pair of Cinderella-like slippers would chassez cross with a brace of thick-soled broghans, in making which, one of the lost feet of the Colossus of Rhodes may have served for a last. Those raven locks, dressed a la Madonne, over eyes of jet, and touching a cheek where blood of a deeper hue, mingling with the less glowing current from European veins, tell of a lineage drawn from the original owners of the soil; while these golden tresses, floating away from eyes of heaven's own colour over a neck of alabaster, recall the Gothic ancestry of some of "England's born." How piquantly do these trim and beaded leggins peep from under that simple dress of black, as its tall, nut-brown wearer moves, as if unconsciously, through the graceful mazes of the dance. How divertingly do those inflated gigots, rising like wind-sails from the little Dutch-built hull, jar against those tall plumes which impend over them like a commodore's pennant on the same vessel. But what boots all these incongruities, when the spirit of festive good humour animates every one present. "It takes all kinds of people to make a world" (as I hear it judiciously observed this side of the mountains), and why should not all these kinds of people be represented as well in a ball-room as in a legislature?

At all events, if I wished to give an intelligent foreigner a favourable opinion of the manners, and deportment of my countrymen in the aggregate, I should not wish a better opportunity, after explaining to him the materials of which it was composed, and the mode in which they were brought together from every section of the Union, than was afforded by this very ball.

"This is a scene of enchantment to me, sir," observed an officer to me, recently exchanged to this post, and formerly stationed here. "There were but a few traders around the fort when I last visited Chicago, and now I can't contrive where the devil all these well-dressed people have come from!"

In many towns of America in the 19th century, there were traveling dancing-masters who taught the quadrille, a dance in quadrangular formation, and square dances, which were dances done in square formation. These dancing-masters, or indeed any who knew the dances, would teach jigs from Ireland, reels from Scotland, quadrilles from France, and hornpipes from England.

The more religious communities, of which there were many, did not allow dancing. As a substitute, games became the social diversion. The games were group movements made to sung words. These sung words became songs and are known as play-party songs. After a time rhythmic popular songs like "Old Dan Tucker," "Buffalo Gals," "Zip Coon," were borrowed for this purpose. The songs were catchy and provided an easy verse form to which new lines could be made up.

Davy Crockett used to say after a frontier dance, "It would do you good to see our boys and girls dancing. None of your straddling, mincing, sadying; but a regular sifter, cut-the-buckle, chicken-flutter, set-to."

Dr. Sam, my uncle, had a different feeling about dancing, especially of the minuet which he hated, "The men look as if they were hired to do it and were doubtful of being paid."

77

KISSING IN THE UNITED STATES

I have been collecting kissing data from newspapers all over the United States. . . .

Boston Transcript: When a wild lark attempts to steal a kiss from a Nantucket girl, she says, "Come sheer off, or I'll split your mainsail with a typhoon." The Boston girls hold still until they are well kissed, when they flare up and say, "I think you ought to be ashamed."

Irwinton Herald: When a young chap steals a kiss from an Alabama girl, she says, "I reckon it's my time now," and gives him a box on the ear that he don't forget in a week.

New Orleans Picayune: When a clever fellow steals a kiss from a Louisiana girl, she smiles, blushes deeply, and says— nothing. We think our girls have more taste and sense than those of down East and Alabama. When a man is smart enough to steal the divine luxury from them, they are perfectly satisfied.

Lynn Record: When a female is here saluted with a buss, she puts on her bonnet and shawl, answereth thus,—"I am astonished at thy assurance, Jedediah; for this indignity I will sew thee up."

Bungtown Chronicle: The ladies in this village receive a salute with Christian meekness: they follow the Scripture rule,— when smitten on the one cheek they turn the other also.

New York Evening Star: When a Bergen girl gets kissed she very calmly remarks, "Hans, tat ish good"; and when a Block Island girl receives a buss, she exclaims with considerable animation, "Well, John, you've wiped my chaps off beautiful."

CHARLES DICKENS: BY STEAMBOAT
TO CINCINNATI

Charles Dickens traveled West by all means of transportation: coach, horse, canal boat and steamboat—1842. His most harrowing experience was on the Ohio River by steamboat from Pittsburgh to Cincinnati. His experience is well worth reading.

Our next point was Cincinnati: and as this was a steamboat journey, and western steamboats usually blow up one or two a week in the season, it was advisable to collect opinions in reference to the comparative safety of the vessels bound that way, then lying in the river. One called the *Messenger* was the best recommended.

The *Messenger* was one among a crowd of high-pressure steamboats, clustered together by a wharf-side, which, looked down upon from the rising ground that forms the landing-place, and backed by the lofty bank on the opposite side of the river, appeared no larger than so many floating models. She had some forty passengers on board, exclusive of the poorer persons on the lower deck; and in half an hour, or less, proceeded on her way.

We had, for ourselves, a tiny state-room with two berths in it, opening out of the ladies' cabin. There was, undoubtedly, something satisfactory in this "location," inasmuch as it was the stern, and we had been a great many times very gravely recommended to keep as far aft as possible, "because the steamboats generally blew up forward." Nor was this an unnecessary caution, as the occurrence and circumstances of more than one such fatality during our stay sufficiently testified. Apart from this source of self-congratulations, it was an unspeakable relief to have any place, no matter how confined, where one could be alone.

If the native packets I have already described be unlike anything we are in the habit of seeing on water, these western vessels are still more foreign to all the ideas we are accustomed to entertain of boats. I hardly know what to liken them to, or how to describe them.

In the first place, they have no mast, cordage, tackle, rigging, or other such boat-like gear; nor have they anything in their shape at all calculated to remind one of a boat's head, stern, sides, or keel. Except that they are in the water, and display a couple of paddle-boxes, they might be intended, for anything that appears to the contrary, to perform some unknown service, high and dry, upon a mountain top. There is no visible deck, even: nothing but a long, black, ugly roof, covered with burnt-out feathery sparks; above which tower two iron chimneys, and a hoarse escape valve, and a glass steerage-house. Then, in order as the eye descends toward the water, are the sides, and doors, and windows of the state-rooms, jumbled as oddly together as though they formed a small street, built by the varying tastes of a dozen men: the whole is supported on beams and pillars resting on a dirty barge, but a few inches above the water's edge: and in the narrow space between this upper structure and this barge's deck, are the furnace fires and machinery, open at the sides to every wind that blows, and every storm of rain it drives along its path.

Passing one of these boats at night, and seeing the great body of fire, exposed as I have just described, that rages and roars beneath the frail pile of painted wood: the machinery, not warded off or guarded in any way, but doing its work in the midst of the crowd of idlers and emigrants

246

and children, who throng the lower deck: under the management, too, of reckless men whose acquaintance with its mysteries may have been of six months' standing: one feels directly that the wonder is, not that there should be so many fatal accidents, but that any journey should be safely made.

Within, there is one long narrow cabin, the whole length of the boat; from which the state-rooms open, on both sides. A small portion of it at the stern is partitioned off for the ladies; and the bar is at the opposite extreme. There is a long table down the centre, and at either end a stove. The washing apparatus is forward, on the deck. It is a little better than on board the canal boat, but not much. In all modes of travelling, the American customs, with reference to the means of personal cleanliness and wholesome ablution, are extremely negligent and filthy.

We are to be on board the *Messenger* three days: arriving at Cincinnati (barring accidents) on Monday morning. There are three meals a day. Breakfast at seven, dinner at half-past twelve, supper about six. At each, there are a great many small dishes and plates upon the table, with very little in them; so that although there is every appearance of a mighty "spread," there is seldom really more than a joint: except for those who fancy slices of beet-root, shreds of dried beef, complicated entanglements of yellow pickle, maize, Indian corn, apple-sauce, and pumpkin.

Some people fancy all these little dainties together (and sweet preserves beside), by way of relish to their roast pig. They are generally those dyspeptic ladies and gentlemen who eat unheard-of quantities of hot corn bread (almost as good for the digestion as a kneaded pin-cushion), for breakfast, and for supper. Those who do not observe this custom, and who help themselves several times instead, usually suck their knives and forks meditatively, until they have decided what to take next: then pull them out of their mouths: put them in the dish; help themselves; and fall to work again. At dinner, there is nothing to drink upon the table, but great jugs full of cold water. Nobody says anything, at any meal, to anybody. All the passengers are very dismal, and seem to have tremendous secrets weighing on their minds. There is no conversation, no laughter, no cheerfulness, no sociality, except in spitting; and that is done in silent fellowship round the stove, when the meal is over. Every man sits down, dull and languid; swallows his fare as if breakfasts, dinners, and suppers, were necessities of nature never to be coupled with recreation or enjoyment; and having bolted his food in a gloomy silence, bolts himself, in the same state. But for these animal observances, you might suppose the whole male portion of the company to be the melancholy ghosts of departed bookkeepers, who had fallen dead at the desk: such is their weary air of business and calculation. Undertakers on duty would be sprightly beside them; and a collation of funeral-baked meats, in comparison with these meals would be a sparkling festivity. . . .

79

DICKENS: ON SPITTOONS

Charles Dickens, as an observer of the American scene, had many pointed observations to make. However, one American habit revolted him beyond all.

As Washington may be called the headquarters of tobacco-tinctured saliva, the time is come when I must confess, without any disguise, that the prevalence of those two odious practices of chewing and expectorating began about this time to be anything but agreeable, and soon became most offensive and sickening. In all the public places of America, this filthy custom is recognized. In the courts of law, the judge has his spittoon, the crier his, the witness his, and the prisoner his; while the jurymen and spectators are provided for, as so many men who in the course of nature must desire to spit incessantly. In the hospitals, the students of medicine are requested, by notices upon the wall, to eject their tobacco juice into the boxes provided for that purpose, and not to discolour the stairs. In public buildings, visitors are implored, through the same agency, to squirt the essence of their quids, or "plugs," as I have heard them called by gentlemen learned in this kind of sweetmeat, into the national spittoons, and not about the bases of the marble columns. But in some parts, this custom is inseparably mixed up with every meal and morning call, and with all the transactions of social life. The stranger, who follows in the track I took myself, will find it in its full bloom and glory, luxuriant in all its alarming recklessness, at Washington. And let him not persuade himself (as I once did, to my shame) that previous tourists have exaggerated its extent. The thing itself is an exaggeration of nastiness, which cannot be outdone. . . .

ACROSS AMERICA

The exciting promise of open land ever westward led to the establishment of a succession of frontiers—as one became comparatively civilized, another section of land was opened up. People moved westward on foot, by horseback, by stage and on horse-carts. Henry Fearon, in his *Narrative of a Journey of Five Thousand Miles Through America,* wrote:

The progress of the stage was so slow and painful, that I preferred walking; this afforded me an opportunity to entering into the views and little histories of fellow-travelers. No person here need feel backward in asking questions, and all answer without hesitation or reserve. The women I found the most communicative; their husband being chiefly engaged in dragging along their wretched nags. The first I conversed with was from Jersey, out 32 days; she was sitting upon a log, which served for the double purpose of a seat and a fire; their wagon had broken down the day before; her husband was with it at a distant blacksmith's; she had been seated there all night, her last words went to my heart: "Ah, Sir, I wish to God we had never left home."

Another of the many Englishmen who came to America to travel and observe and returned to London to write of it was James Flint. He describes most vividly what the westward flow of traffic was like and tells how at one point he came up with a party of travelers consisting of a man, his wife and their ten children:

The eldest of the progeny had the youngest tied to his back; and the father pushed a wheelbarrow, containing the moveables of the family. They were removing from New Jersey to the State of Ohio, a land journey of 340 miles to Pittsburgh. Abrupt edges of rocks, higher than the wheel, occasionally interrupted the passage. Their humble carriage must be lifted over these. A little farther onward we passed a young woman, carrying a sucking child in her arms, and leading a very little one by the hand. It is impossible to take particular notice of all the travellers on the way. We could scarcely look before or behind, without seeing some of them. The Canterbury pilgrims were not so diversified nor so interesting as these.

A little further on, this same James Flint was traveling by coach from Philadelphia to Pittsburgh. Let his diary entry of September 21, 1818, speak for him:

At Chambersburg the coach halted during the night. The rough roads already surmounted, and the report of worse still before us, determined two of the passengers, besides myself, to walk, as an easier mode of travelling over the mountains. Chambersburg is 143 miles from Philadelphia, and 155 from Pittsburgh; and lies in the intersection of the roads from York, Baltimore, and Philadelphia. Several branches of what has been very properly called the current of emigration, being here united, strangers from the eastern country, and from Europe, are passing in an unceasing train. An intelligent gentleman, at this place, informed me, that this stream of emigration has flowed more copiously this year, than at any former period; and that the people now moving westward, are ten times more numerous than they were, ten years ago. His computation is founded on the comparative amount of the stage-coach business, and on careful observation. This astonishing statement is, in some degree, countenanced by a late notice in a New York newspaper, that stated the number of emigrants which arrived in that port during the week, ending the 31st of August last, to be 2050.

The gentleman alluded to, says, that shades of character, sensibly different from one another, are forming in the western States. He represents the Kentuckians to be a high-toned people, who frequently announce their country, as if afraid of being mistaken for inhabitants of Ohio State.

A POEM: 1846

LOVE IN THE BOWERY

I seen her on the sidewalk,
   When I run with No. 9:
My eyes spontaneous sought out hern—
   And hern was fixed on mine.
She waved her pocket handkerchief,
   As we went rushin' by—
No boss that ever killed in York
   Was happier than I.
I felt that I had done it;
   And what had won her smile—
'Twas them embroidered braces,
   And that 'ere immortal tile.

I sought her out at Wauxhall,
   Afore that place was shet—
Oh! that happy, happy evenin',
   I recollex it yet.
I gin her cords of peanuts,
   And a apple and a "wet."
Oh! that happy, happy evenin',
   I recollex it yet.

I took her out to Harlem—
　　On the road we cut a swell,
And the nag we had afore us
　　Went twelve mile afore he fell.
And though ven he struck the pavement,
　　The "Crab" began to fail,
I got another mile out—
　　By twisting of his tail.

I took her to the Bowery—
　　She sat long side of me—
They acted out a piece they called,
　　"The Wizard of the Sea,"
And when the sea-fight was fetched on,
　　Eliza cried "hay! hay!"
And like so many minutes there
　　Five hours slipped away.

Before the bridle halter,
　　I thought to call her mine—
The day was fixed when she to me
　　Her hand and heart should jine.
The rum old boss, the father, swore
　　He'd gin her out er hand,
Two hundred cash—and also treat
　　To number 9's men stand.

But bless me! if she didn't slip
　　Her halter on the day;
A peddler from Connecticut,
　　He carried her away.
And when the news was brought to me,
　　I felt almighty blue;
And though I didn't shed no tear,
　　Perhaps I cussed "a few."

Well, let it pass—there's other gals,
   As beautiful as she;
And many a butcher's lovely child
   Has cast sheep's eyes at me.
I wears no crape upon my hat,
   'Cause I'm a packin' sent—
I only takes a extra horn,
   Observing, "LET HER WENT!"

SAN FRANCISCO

Under Spanish rule, San Francisco was known as *Yerba Buena* and was a prosperous commercial town. In 1847, the name was changed in honor of St. Francis.

A German immigrant who had arrived in San Francisco in the fall of 1849 returned for a visit in January, 1850. He was dumb-struck at the material progress which had been made: "I had left tents and low huts and shanties only two months before; and now there were regular streets of high wooden and even here and there, brick buildings. But if the habitations had improved, the streets had become proportionately worse. . . . In going from one house to another you had to wade through mud, and crossing a street seemed a matter of life and death. Many places became really impassable and in Clay and Montgomery Streets, mules were several times drowned in the middle of the road."

YANKEE DOODLE: SAN FRANCISCO

There is no land upon the earth
Contains the same amount of worth;
And he that could not here reside,
Had ought to freeze the other side!

257

    You who don't believe it
    You who don't believe it
    You who don't believe it,
    Come yourselves and see!

We've got more gold than all the world,
A flag that wins when e'er unfurled,
And smarter men to help us through
Than England, France, or Mexico.

We've smarter ships than Johnny Bull,
Larger sheep with finer wool;
A prison too! You cannot fail
To throw a bull through by the tail.

We raise the largest cabbage heads,
Got more and better feather beds;
Of everything we've got the best,
And thieves until you cannot rest.

All ruffianism now is o'er,
The country's safer than before;
Our cities keep the rowdies straight,
Or send them through the golden gate.

We've got the highest mountains here,
Taller trees and faster deer,
And travel more, at higher rates,
Than people in the eastern states.

We've got the smartest river boats,
And, ten to one, old whiskey bloats;
We're blest with very heavy fogs,
And any amount of poodle dogs!

We've got a few unmarried g'hals,
Railroads, ditches and canals;
Although we did repudiate,
A joke 'twas only to create.

To one and all, both young and old,
You're welcome to the land of gold;
So come along, be not afraid,
We guarantee you all well paid!

In 1849, hundreds of tents and buildings were scattered over the heights and along the shore for more than a mile around the curve of San Francisco Bay. Abandoned ships served as warehouses and hotels—great quantities of goods were piled up in the open for want of places to store them. The price of goods and the price of skilled labor had skyrocketed out of sight. It was cheaper to buy a new shirt and throw the dirty one away than to have it washed and ironed. Fastidious folk who had brought fine linen with them and prized it, sent their wash by clipper ship to Canton or Honolulu for laundering.

An Easterner arriving in San Francisco in the summer of 1849, wrote home, "I expected to take up either the ministry or the law but there is neither law nor gospel here. Yet, it is most orderly."

83

THE MINERS' TEN COMMANDMENTS
(Issued in California, 1853)

A man spake these words and said: "I am a miner who wandered from 'a way down East' and came to sojourn in a strange land, and see the elephant. And behold, I saw him and bear witness, that from the key of his trunk to the end of his tail, his whole body has passed before me; and I followed him until his huge feet stood still before a clapboard shanty; then with his trunk extended he pointed to a candle card tacked upon a shingle, as though he would say 'Read,' and I read the

MINERS' TEN COMMANDMENTS

ONE. Thou shalt have no other claim but one.

TWO. Thou shalt not make unto thyself any false claim, nor any likeness to a mean man by jumping one, whatever thou findest on the top above or on the rock beneath, or in a crevice underneath the rock:—or I will visit the miners around to invite them on my side, and when they decide against thee, thou shalt take thy pick and thy pan, thy shovel and thy blankets, with all that thou hast, and 'go prospecting' to seek good diggings but thou shalt find none. Then, when thou hast returned, in sorrow shalt thou find that thine old claim is worked out, yet no pile made thee to hide in the ground, or in an old boot beneath thy bunk, or in buckskin or bottle underneath thy cabin; but hast paid all that was in thy purse away, worn out thy boots and thy garments so that there is nothing good about them but the pockets, and thy patience is likened unto thy garments; and at last thou shalt hire thy body out to make thy board and save thy bacon.

THREE. Thou shalt not go prospecting before thy claim gives out. Neither shalt thou take thy money, nor thy gold dust, nor thy good name to the gaming table in vain; for monte, twenty-one, roulette, faro, lansquenet, and poker will prove to thee that the more thou puttest down the less thou shalt take up; and when thou thinkest of thy wife and children, thou shalt not hold thyself guiltless—but insane.

FOUR. Thou shalt not remember what thy friends do at home on the Sabbath Day, lest the remembrance may not compare favorably with what thou doest here—Six days thou mayest pick or dig all that thy body can stand under; but the other day is Sunday; yet thou mayest wash all thy dirty shirts, darnest all thy stockings, tap thy boots, mend thy clothing, chop the whole week's firewood, make up and bake thy bread, and boil thy pork and beans, that thou wait not when thou returnest from thy long toil weary. For in six days labour only thou canst not work enough to wear out thy body in two years; but if thy workest hard on Sunday also, thou canst do it in six months; and thou and thy son and thy daughter, thy male friend and thy female friend, thy morals and thy conscience, be none the better for it; but reproach thee shouldst thou ever return with thy worn-out body to thy mother's fireside; and thou shalt not strive to justify thyself, because the trader and the blacksmith, the carpenter and the merchant, the tailors, Jews, and buccanneers defy God and civilization by keeping not the Sabbath Day nor wish for a day of rest, such as memory, youth, and home made hallowed.

FIVE. Thou shalt not think more of all thy gold and

how thou canst make it fastest, than how thou wilt enjoy it, after thou hast ridden roughshod over thy good old parents' precepts and examples, that thou mayest have nothing to reproach, and sting thee when thou art left ALONE in the land where thy father's blessing and thy mother's love hath sent thee.

SIX. Thou shalt not kill thy body by working in the rain, even though thou shalt make enough to buy physic and attendance with. Neither shalt thou kill thy neighbor's body in a duel; for by 'keeping cool,' thou canst save his life and thy conscience. Neither shalt thou destroy thyself by getting 'tight' nor 'stewed' nor 'high' nor 'corned' nor 'half sheets over' nor 'three sheets to the wind' by drinking smoothly down 'brandy slings,' 'gin cocktails,' 'whiskey punches,' 'rum toddies,' nor 'egg nogs.' Neither shalt thou suck 'mint juleps' nor 'sherry cobblers' through a straw nor gurgle from a bottle the 'raw material' nor 'take it neat' from the decanter; for while thou art swallowing down thy purse, and thy coat from thy back, thou art burning the coat from off thy stomach; and if thou couldst see the houses and lands, and gold dust and home comforts already lying there—a huge pile—thou shouldst feel a choking in thy throat: and when to that thou addest thy crooked walkings and hiccuping talkings of lodgings in the gutter, of broilings in the sun, of prospect holes half full of water and of shafts and ditches from which thou hast emerged like a drowning rat, thou wilt feel disgusted with thyself and inquire, 'Is thy servant a dog that he doeth these things?' verily I will say. Farewell old bottle, I will kiss thy gurgling lips no more. And thou, slings, cocktails, punches, smashes, cobblers, nogs, toddies, sangerees, and juleps, forever farewell. Thy remembrance shames me; henceforth, 'I cut thy acquaintance,' and headaches, tremblings, heart burnings, blue devils, and all the unholy catalogue of evils that follov in thy train. My wife's smiles and my children's merry-hearted laugh shall charm and reward me for having the manly firmness and courage to say NO. I wish thee an eternal farewell.

SEVEN. Thou shalt not grow discouraged, nor think of going home before thou hast made thy 'pile' because thou hast not 'struck a lead' nor found a rich 'crevice' nor sunk a hole upon a 'pocket' lest in going home thou shalt leave four dollars a day, and go to work, ashamed, at fifty cents, and serve thee right, for thou knowest by staying here, thou mightest strike a lead and fifty dollars a day, and keep thy manly self-respect and then go home with enough to make thyself and others happy.

EIGHT. Thou shalt not steal a pick nor a shovel, nor a pan from a fellow miner nor take away his tools without his leave; nor borrow those he cannot spare, nor return them broken nor trouble him to fetch them back again, nor talk to him while his water rent is running on, nor remove his stake to enlarge thy claim, nor undermine his bank in following a lead, nor pan out gold from his riffle box, nor wash the 'tailings' from his share's mouth. Neither shalt thou pick out specimens from the company's pan to put them in thy mouth or in thy purse nor cheat thy partner of his share; nor steal from thy cabin-mate his gold dust to add to thine for he will be sure to discover what thou hast done and will straightaway call his fellow miners together and if the law hinder them not, they will hang thee or give fifty lashes or shave thy head and brand thee, like a horse thief, with 'R' upon thy cheek to be known and read of all men, Californians in particular.

NINE. Thou shalt not tell any false tales about 'good diggings in the mountains' to thy neighbor, that thou mayest benefit a friend who hath mules and provisions and tools and blankets he cannot sell—lest in deceiving thy neighbor, when he returneth through the snow with naught save his rifle, he present thee with the contents thereof and like a dog, thou shalt fall down and die.

TEN. Thou shalt not commit unsuitable matrimony nor

covet 'single blessedness' nor forget about maidens nor neglect thy 'first love'—but thou shalt consider how faithfully and patiently she awaiteth thy return; yes, and covereth each epistle that thou sendest with kisses of kindly welcome—until she hath thyself. Neither shalt thou covet thy neighbor's wife, nor trifle with the affections of his daughter; yet, if thy heart be free and thou dost love and covet each other, thou shalt 'pop the question' like a man lest another, more manly than thou art, should step in before thee and thou love her in vain and in the anguish of thy heart a disappointment, thou shalt quote the language of the great and say 'sich is life' and thy future lot be that of a poor, lonely, despised, and comfortless bachelor.

A new commandment give I unto thee—if thou hast a wife and little ones, that thou lovest dearer than life—that thou keep them continually before thee, to cheer and urge thee onward until thou canst say, 'I have enough—God bless them—I will return.' Then, as thou journiest toward thy much loved home with open arms shall they come forth to welcome thee and, falling upon thy neck weep tears of unutterable joy that thou art come; then in the fullness of thy heart's gratitude thou shalt kneel together before thy Heavenly Father to thank Him for thy safe return. AMEN— So mote it be.

THE FRONTIER

The American frontier was many things and the surprising thing was that, as Dr. Sam said, "Them frontiersmen warn't born in the wood to be scared by an owl!" Because, like many men who traveled without attempting to either settle, fight the Indians, or look for gold, he had a great respect for those who did.

Continuing the tradition of translating into song the many experiences in which they participated, little song books were printed that were like the early broadsides, reflecting the experiences of miners, buffalo skinners, or would-be settlers.

THE LITTLE OLD SOD SHANTY ON THE PLAIN
THE STORY OF THE UNHAPPY MINER

> My happy days are past,
> The mines have failed at last,
> The canyons and gulches no longer will pay,
> There's nothing left for me,
> I'll never, never see
> My happy, happy home far away.
>
> I mine from break of day,
> But cannot make it pay,
> Disheartened return to my cabin at night,

Where rattlesnakes crawl round
My bed made on the ground,
And, coiling up, lay ready to bite.

My poor old leaky lamp
Is always cold and damp;
My blanket is covered with something
    that crawls:
My bread will never rise,
My coffee-pot capsize.
I'd rather live inside of prison walls.

My boots are full of holes,
Like merchants, have no *soles*;
My hands, once so soft, are harder
    than stone;
My pants and woolen shirt
Are only rags and dirt;
And must I live and die here alone?

It's "Starve or pay the dust,"
For merchants will not trust,
And then in the summer the diggings
    are dry;
Of course then I am broke,
Swelled up by poison oak;
It's even so, I really would not lie.

I've lived on pork and beans,
Through all those trying scenes,
So long I dare not look a hog in the face;
And often do I dream
Of custard pies and cream;
But really it is a *quien sabe* case.

If I were home again,
To see green fields of grain,
And all kinds of fruit hanging ripe
   on the trees;
I there would live and die,
The gold mines bid goodby—
Forever free from bed-bugs and fleas.

THE STORY OF THE BUFFALO SKINNERS

'Twas in the town of Jacksboro in the spring of seventy-three,
A man by the name of Crego came stepping up to me,
Saying, "How do you do, young fellow, and how would you
   like to go
And spend one summer pleasantly on the range of the Buffalo?"

"It's me being out of employment," this to Crego I did say,
"This going out on the buffalo range depends upon the pay.
But if you will pay good wages and transportation too,
I think, sir, I will go with you to the range of the buffalo."

"Yes, I will pay good wages, give transportation too,
Provided you will go with me and stay the summer through;
But if you should grow homesick, come back to Jacksboro,
I won't pay transportation from the range of the buffalo.

It's now our outfit was complete, seven able-bodied men,
With navy six and needle gun, our troubles did begin.
Our way it was a pleasant one, the route we had to go
Until we crossed Pease River on the range of the Buffalo.

It's now we've crossed Pease River, our troubles have begun.
The first damned tail I went to rip, Christ! How I cut my
   thumb!

While skinning the damned old stinkers our lives wasn't a show
For the Indians watched to pick us off while skinning the
buffalo.

He fed us on such sorry chuck I wished myself most dead,
It was old jerked beef, croton coffee, and sour bread.
Pease River's as salt as hell fire, the water I could never go—
O God! I wished I had never come to the range of the buffalo.

Our meat it was buffalo hump and iron wedge bread
And all we had to sleep on was a buffalo robe for a bed;
The fleas and greybacks worked on us, O boys, it was not slow,
I'll tell you there's no worse hell on earth than the range of the
buffalo.

Our hearts were cased with buffalo hocks, our souls were cased
with steel,
And the hardships of that summer would nearly make us reel.
While skinning the damned old stinkers our lives they had
no show,
For the Indians waited to pick us off on the hills of Mexico.

The season being near over, old Crego he did say
The crowd had been extravagant, was in debt to him that day,
We coaxed him and we begged him and still it was no go,
We left old Crego's bones to bleach on the range of the buffalo.

Oh, it's now we've crossed the Pease River and homeward we
are bound,
No more in that hell fired country shall ever we be found.
Go home to our wives and sweethearts, tell others not to go,
For God's forsaken the buffalo range and the damned old
buffalo.

I crossed the Missouri and joined a large train
Which bore us o'er mountain and valley and plain;
And often of evenings out hunting we'd go
To shoot the fleet antelope and wild buffalo.

Without any money provisions to buy
We'd sneak around the hills shooting elk on the sly,
We'd shoot the fat deer and take him to town
To buy flour to bake bread and tea a few pound.

We heard of Sioux Indians, all out on the plains,
A-killing poor drivers and burning their trains—
A-killing poor drivers with arrows and bow,
When captured by Indians no mercy they'd show.

We travelled three weeks till we came to the Platte
And pitched out our tents at the head of the flat;
We spread down our blankets on the green grassy ground,
While our horses and oxen were a-grazing around.

While taking refreshments we heard a low yell,
The whoop of Sioux Indians coming up from the dell
We sprang to our rifles with a flash in each eye
"Boys," says our brave leader, "we'll fight till we die."

We gathered our horses, got ready to fight,
As the band of Sioux Indians just came into sight,
They came down upon us with a whoop and a yell,
At the crack of our rifles, oh six of them fell.

They made a bold dash and came near to our train
And the arrows fell round us like hail and like rain
But with our long rifles we fed them cold lead
Till many a brave warrior around us lay dead.

With our small band there were just twenty-four,
And of the Sioux Indians there were five hundred or more;
We fought them with courage; we spoke not a word,
Till the end of the battle that was all that was heard.

We shot their bold chief at the head of the band;
He died like a warrior with a gun in his hand.
When they saw their bold chief layin' dead in his gore,
They whooped and they yelled, and we saw them no more.

We hitched up our horses and started our train
Three more bloody battles this trip on the plain,
And in our last battle three of our brave boys did fell
And we left them to rest in a green shady dell.

We travelled by day, guarded camp during night,
Till Oregon's mountains looked high in their might.
Now at Pocahontas beside a clear stream
Our journey is ended in the land of our dream. . . .

And then there is the story of *"Joe Bowers and the Red-
headed Baby"*:

> My name is Joe Bowers,
> And I've got a brother Ike;
> I'm just here from old Missouri,
> And all the way from Pike;
> I tell you why I left there and why I began to roam,
> And left my aged parents,
> So far away from home.
>
> I used to court a gal there;
> Her name was Sallie Black;
> I asked her if she'd marry me,
> She said it was a whack;
> Says she to me,

"Joe Bowers, before we're hitched for life,
You ought to get a little home
To keep your little wife."

Says I, "My dearest Sally,
O Sally, for your sake,
I'll go to California
And try to raise a stake."
Says she to me, "Joe Bowers,
You are the one to win."
She gave me a kiss to seal the bargain—
And I throwed a dozen in.

I'll never forget my feelings
When I bid adieu to all.
Sal, she cotched me round the neck
And I began to bawl.
When I began they all commenced,
You never heard the like,
How they all took on and cried and cried
The day I left old Pike.

When I got to this country,
I had nary a red,
I had such wolfish feelings,
That I wished myself most dead.
But the thoughts of my dear Sally
Soon made this feeling git:
And whispered hopes to Bowers,
Lord I wish I had 'em yit.

At last I went to mining,
Put in my biggest licks,
Come down upon the boulders
Just like a thousand bricks.

I worked both late and early
In rain and sun and snow,
I was working for my Sally,
It was all the same to Joe.

85

DAVY ON THE MISSOURI

"That Davy Crockett sure was a keel-boat man!" my uncle,
Dr. Sam, would say when the family would sit around talking
of my grandparents or my uncles who were frontiersmen of
physical strength and the kind of wit we associate only with
frontier life. They felt a great kinship with Crockett and his
rough but pointed epigrams.

Crockett's experience with the flatboat men of the Missouri
fascinated us all. He was once part-owner of a flatboat but
turned out to be ill-suited to life on the river. On his first trip
toward New Orleans, he wrecked his boat on a bar in the Mississippi and it began to sink fast. The redoubtable bear hunter
was caught tight in the tiny cabin which had only one small
window, far too small for Davy's heft. A fellow boatman yanked
him free just as he was gurgling a premature goodbye.

He came out of the experience with his life but little else.
"Lost most of my clothes, a good part of my skin and all of my
investment. Only don't forget I'm the man that, single-handed,
towed the broadhorn over a sand bar—the identical infant who
girdled a hickory by smiling at the bark: and if anyone denies
it let him make his will and pay the expenses of a funeral."

JOKES: CIRCA 1860

1. *A Civil War Joke:* During the War of the Rebellion, a merchant of Milwaukee, who is an excellent hand at sketching, drew most admirably on the wall of his store a Negro's head, and underneath it wrote, in a manner worthy of the Delphic oracle, "Dis-Union for eber." Whether the sentence meant loyalty to the Union or not, was the puzzling question which the gentleman himself never answered, invariably stating to the inquirers, "Read it for yourselves, gentlemen." So from that day to this, as the saying goes, "no one knows how dat darkey stood on de war question."

2. *A Female Joke:* Another question is puzzling the young ladies who attend a female college. Some person had written on the outer wall of the college, "Young women should set good examples; for young men will follow them." The question that is now perplexing the heads of several of the young ladies of the college is, whether the writer meant what he or she (the handwriting was rather masculine) wrote, in a moral sense or in an ironical one.

3. At a very learned discussion on strata, the other day, at the house of Professor Agassiz, Mr. Brown asked if there were any strata of precious gems.

"No, none whatever," replied the professor.

"I've heard of one," said Mr. Brown.

"Impossible!" was the rejoinder.

"Oh, yes," said Mr. Brown, "and it was called a *stratagem!*"

THE MORMONS BOLD

The Mormon people today are famous for their church choirs all over the world. It is as if they are a people able to express themselves through song. And it seems to have been so in their early days, for not only did their people write many beautiful hymns but they wrote folk songs that tell a great deal about their courage, their fears, and their ability to laugh.

Take that momentous trek across the Great Plains into Utah when persecuted, insufficiently supplied with basic necessities, they wandered looking for the valley of hope promised to them by their leader. Here is what they sang as they walked day after day, pulling their poor possessions along:

> Oh, some must push and some must pull,
> As we go marching up the hill,
> So merrily on our way we go,
> Until we reach the valley, O!

> Ye saints who dwell on Europe's shore,
> Prepare yourself for many more,
> To leave behind your native land,
> For sure God's Judgments are at hand.

For you must cross the raging main,
Before the promised land you gain,
And with the faithful make a start
To cross the plains with your hand cart.

The lands that boast of modern light,
We know are all as dark as night,
Where poor men toil and want for bread,
Where peasant hosts are blindly led.

These lands that boast of liberty,
You ne'er again would wish to see,
When you from Europe make a start
To cross the plains with your hand cart.

As on the roads the carts are pulled,
'Twould very much surprise the world,
To see the old and feeble dame
Thus lend a hand to pull the same.

And maidens fair will dance and sing,
Young men as happy as a king.
And children too will laugh and play,
Their strength increasing day by day.

But some will say it is too bad
The saints upon the foot to pad.
And more than that to pull a load,
As they go marching o'er the road.

But then we say it is the plan
To gather up the best of men,
And women too for none but they
Will ever travel in this way.

And long before the valley's gained,
We will be met upon the plains,
With music sweet and friends so dear,
And fresh supplies our hearts to cheer.

And then with music and with song
How cheerfully we'll march along,
And thank the day we made a start
To cross the plains in our hand carts.

When you get there among the rest
Obedient be and you'll be blest,
And in God's chambers be shut in
With judgments cleanse the earth from sin.

For we do know it will be so,
God's servants spoke it long ago,
We say it is high time to start
To cross the plains with our hand cart.

Later, when Salt Lake City was flourishing and that salt
valley had been made to flourish by the toil of Mormon hands,
the Union Railroad decided to put its lines through the flats
of Utah. This meant the end of Mormon isolation. To the
Mormon people it also meant the infusion of alien ideas and
of people who were not themselves Mormon. Someone put this
feeling into a satirical song written in 1868, "The Utah Iron
Horse":

The Iron Horse draws nigh
With its smoke nostrils high,
Eating fire while he grazeth,
Drinking water while he blazeth,
Then the steam forces out,
Whistles loud clear the route
For the Iron Horse is coming
With a train in his wake.

We have isolated been,
But soon we shall be seen
Thru this White Mountain region
Folk can learn of our religion.
Count each man, many wives,
How they're held in their hives,
And see those dreadful dives,
How they lynch many lives.

If alive we shall be,
Many folks we shall see,
Nobles, lords, flotsam, beggars,
Among us will come the slavers.
Saints will come, sinners too.
We'll have all that we can do,
For this great Union Railroad
It will fetch the Devil through.

And this did not end their ability to laugh, even at themselves. With saving humor they were able to create and sing
about polygamy and their beloved leader:

Brigham Young was a Mormon bold,
And a leader of the roaring rams,
And a shepherd of a heap of pretty little sheep
And a nice fold of pretty little lambs.

(Chorus)
Brigham, Brigham Young 'tis a miracle he survived,
With his roaring rams, his pretty little lambs
And five and forty wives.

And he lived with five and forty wives,
In the city of Great Salt Lake,
Where they woo and coo as pretty doves do,
And cackle like ducks to a drake.

Number forty-five was about sixteen,
Number one was sixty-three,
And among such a riot how he ever keeps them quiet,
Is a right down mystery to me.

For they clatter and they claw, and they jaw, jaw, jaw,
Each one has a different desire,
It would aid the reknown of the best shop in town,
To supply them with half what they require.

Oh, Brigham Young was a stout man once,
But now he is thin and old,
And I love to state there's no hair on his pate,
That once wore a covering of gold.

But his youngest wife won't have white wool,
And his old ones won't take red,
So in tearing it out they have taken turn about,
Till they pulled all the wool from his head.

Now his boys they all sing songs all day,
And his girls they all do sums,
And among such a crowd he had it pretty loud,
For there was music and a Chinese gong.

And when they advanced for a Mormon dance,
He is filled with the greatest surprise,
For they're sure to end the night with a Tabernacle fight,
And scratch out one another's eyes.

There never was a house like Brigham Young's,
So curious and so queer,
For his wives were doubled, he had a terrible lot of trouble,
And it gained on him year by year.

He sits in his state and bears his fate,
In a sanctified sort of way.
He has one wife to bury and one wife to marry,
And a new kid born every day.

Now if anybody envies Brigham Young,
Let him go to Great Salt Lake,
And if they have leisure to examine at their pleasure,
They'll find it's a great mistake.

One wife at a time so says my rhyme,
Is enough for the proudest Don,
So e'er you strive to live Lord of forty-five,
Live happy if you can with one.

   (Chorus)
   Brigham, Brigham Young 'tis a miracle he survived,
   With his roaring rams, his pretty little lambs
   And five and forty wives.

SOME NINETEENTH-CENTURY EPITAPHS

IN EAST HARTFORD, CONN.

Now she is dead and cannot stir;
　　Her cheeks are like the faded rose;
Which of us next shall follow her,
　　The Lord Almighty only knows.

Hark, she bids all her friends adieu;
　　An angel calls her to the spheres;
Our eyes the radiant saint pursue
　　Through liquid telescopes of tears.

ON A TOMBSTONE IN NEW JERSEY

Reader, pass on!—don't waste your time
On bad biography and bitter rhyme;
For what I am, this crumbling clay insures,
And what I was, is no affair of yours.

The following illustrated epitaph is copied from a tombstone near Williamsport, Pa.

Sacred to the memory of
HENRY HARRIS
Born June 27th, 1821, of Henry Harris
and Jane, his wife
Died on the 4th of May, 1837, by a kick of a colt
in his bowels.
Peaceable and quiet, a friend to
his father and mother, and respected
by all who knew him, and went
to the world where horses
don't kick, where sorrows and weeping
is no more.

IN A NEW ENGLAND GRAVEYARD

Here lies John Auricular,
Who in the ways of the Lord walked perpendicular

ON LILL

Here liest the tongue of Godfrey Lill,
Which always lied, and lies here still.

THORPE'S CORPSE

ON A SAN FRANCISCO MONEY-LENDER

Here lies old thirty-five per cent:
The more he made, the more he lent;
The more he got, the more he craved;
The more he made, the more he shaved;
Great God! can such a soul be saved?

IN A PENNSYLVANIA GRAVEYARD

Wherever you may be,
    Let your wind blow free;
For the holding of it,
    Was the killing of me.

Here lies the body of John Cole,
His master loved him like his soul;
He could rake hay, none could rake faster
Except that raking dog, his master.

ANDREW JACKSON'S EPITAPH ON HIS WIFE

Here lie the remains of Mrs. Rachel Jackson, wife of President Jackson, who died December 22d, 1828, aged 61. Her face was fair, her person pleasing, her temper amiable, and her heart kind. She delighted in relieving the wants of her fellow creatures, and cultivated that divine pleasure by the most liberal and unpretending methods. To the poor she was a benefactress; to the rich she was an example; to the wretched a comforter; to the prosperous an ornament. Her pity went hand in hand with her benevolence; and she thanked her Creator for being permitted to do good. A being so gentle and yet so virtuous, slander might wound, but could not dishonor. Even death, when he tore her from the arms of her husband, could but transplant her to the bosom of her God.

ON A CONNECTICUT MAN WITH A REMARKABLE TUMOR

Our father lies beneath the sod,
His spirit's gone unto his God;
We never more shall hear his tread,
Nor see the wen upon his head.

John
Burns

Dr. Sam said of this: "Most men suffer enough above ground without being bunglingly abused, post-mortem, in ill-written inscriptions which were at least intended to be civil. We suppose the words were simply intended to record the man's name; but they look marvelously like a noun substantive coupled with a verb in the indicative mood, and affording a sad indication that John burns. There is no hint that John deserved the fate to which he appears to have been consigned since his decease, and we can only say as we read the startling declaration, we should be very sorry to believe it."

BE MY VALENTINE!

O lovely maid, thou art the fairest in all God's mart!
One kiss I send, to pierce, like fire, thy too reluctant heart.
Those charms to win, with all my empire I would gladly part.

CUPID'S BOW AND ARROW

What shape should a love triplet have but that of Cupid's bow and arrow. Read the bow as the first line, the string as the second, and the arrow aimed at the heart of the poet's love as the third line.

Your face,	your tongue,	your wit,
So fair,	so sweet,	so sharp,
First bent,	then drew,	then hit,
Mine eye,	mine ear,	my heart,
Mine eye,	mine ear,	my heart,
To like,	to learn,	to love,
Your face,	your tongue,	your wit,
Doth lead,	doth teach,	doth move.
Your face,	your tongue,	your wit,
With beams,	with sound,	with art,
Doth bind,	doth charm,	doth rule,
Mine eye,	mine ear,	my heart.
Mine eye,	mine ear,	my heart,
With life,	with hope,	with skill,
Your face,	your tongue,	your wit,
Doth feed,	doth feast,	doth fill.
O face!	O tongue!	O wit!
With frowns,	with check,	with smart,
Wrong not,	vex not,	wound not,
Mine eye,	mine ear,	my heart.
This eye,	this ear,	this heart,
Shall joy,	shall bend,	shall swear,
Your face,	your tongue,	your wit,
To serve,	to trust,	to fear.

The lines may be read either from left to right, or from above downwards. They may also be read in various directions.

90

RELIGION ON THE FRONTIER

Religion on the frontier quickly became identified with the revivalist camp meeting. Visited by itinerant preachers, the frontiersman went to church as often as possible, both for his religion and as a social event. Actually, the first camp meeting was held in 1801, when the Presbyterians, Methodists, and Baptists held a joint meeting in Kentucky, setting the style for future meetings held every year thereafter, in other parts of Kentucky, Tennessee, and the Carolinas:

The Baptists' cry at the camp meeting was, "Water! Water! Follow your Lord into the water!" The Methodists sang:

> I'll tell you who the Lord likes best
> It is the shouting Methodist!

Here is a description of such a meeting from "The Church Journal":

Hearing that there was to be a great meeting and a good work in progress, I determined to attend. The sermon was really striking and impressive. The people were generally attentive—many tenderly affected—and except that in the extreme part of the house, where I sat, some old tobacco-planters kept up a continual conversation, in a low tone, about tobacco-plants, seasons, etc.

When the preacher came to the application of his discourse, he became exceedingly vehement and boisterous; and I could hear some sounds in the centre of the house which indicated strong emotion. At length a female voice was heard in a piercing cry, which thrilled through me, and affected the whole audience. In a few seconds one and another rose in different parts of the house, in extreme and visible agitation. Casting off bonnets and caps, and raising their folded hands, they shouted to the utmost extent of their voice; and in a few seconds more the whole audience was agitated, as a forest shaken by a mighty wind. The sympathetic wave, commencing at the centre, extended to the extremities; and at length, it reached our corner, and I felt the conscious effort of resistance as necessary as if I had been exposed to the violence of a storm. I saw a few persons through the whole house who escaped the prevailing influence; even careless boys seemed to be arrested, and joined in the general outcry. But what astonished me most of all, was that the old tobacco-planters whom I have mentioned, and who, I am persuaded, had not heard one word of the sermon, were violently agitated. Every muscle in their brawny faces appeared to be in a tremendous motion, and the big tears chased one another down their wrinkled cheeks. Here I saw the power of sympathy. The feeling was real, and was propagated from person to person by mere sound. The feelings expressed were different; for while some uttered the cry of poignant anguish, others shouted in the accents of triumph.

The speaker's voice was soon silenced, and he sat down and gazed on the scene with a complacent smile. When this tumult had lasted a few minutes, another preacher began to sing a soothing yet lively tune, and was quickly joined by some strong female voices near him; and in less than two minutes the storm was hushed, and there was a great calm. I experienced the most sensible relief to my own feelings from the appropriate *music,* for I could not hear the *words* sung. The dishevelled hair was put in order, the peculiarities of the dress adjusted, and no one seemed conscious of any impropriety. Indeed, there is a peculiar luxury in such excitements, especially when tears are shed copiously, as was the case here.

The case of Orville Gardner is interesting because he was referred to in many church journals as "that unfortunately notorious man." He apparently "got religion" while riding on the road to White Plains and did not hesitate to tell his experiences, describing them as follows:

> After I had my dinner I resolved that I would seek the Lord that night. I made a strong resolution; I felt where I stood that perhaps it was the last time the Lord would strive with me. Saturday night, the invitation was given to come forward to the altar—on my shoulders my load of sin—up I went with them, the cross of Christ upon my back. I got up and threw my sins down by the altar. I tried as hard as a man ever did, and I got no religion.
>
> Sunday night I attended with a like result. That night, I could not sleep, my sins looked so bad; they came up on every hand and looked at me; all of the sins of my life crowded upon me, many I should never have thought of, had not the devil brought them before me. I could not sleep; I wiggled and waggled around the bed all night; the Lord was striving with me. Monday morning, I got up and prayed; I did the best I could; I asked the Lord to take away the weight that bore me down so.

The next day a friend came to see Orville and invited him to go over to White Plains.

> Knowing I would be in good company, I concluded to go, thinking he might do me some good. There was little said on the way, but he told me to keep looking for the Saviour;

that I was trying to get religion, and had let everybody know it; the Lord was willing to bless me at any time or any where.

Orville described how the experience descended upon him:

I was riding along, singing a hymn, and in an instant I felt as though I was blessed. I am sure I gave up my soul and body. The first thing I knew, God spoke peace to my soul. It came like a shot—it came like lightning, when I was not anticipating it, and the first I said, "Glory! God bless me." My friend said he knew it; he felt the shock too. We rode against a stone fence two or three times, and came near tumbling on the ground. The change was surprising; the trees looked as if they had been blessed; everything appeared to have been blessed, even the horse and wagon. I felt strong. I could almost fly. Glory to God, this religion is good!

DOWN IN ARKANSAS

Dr. Sam didn't like traveling in Arkansas. He never could get any kind of information. He'd tell you of twenty conversations like this. . . .

DR. SAM. How do you do, stranger?

MOUNTAINEER. Do pretty much as I please, sir.

DR. SAM. Stranger, do you live about here?

MOUNTAINEER. I reckon I don't live anywheres else!

DR. SAM. Well, how long have you lived here?

MOUNTAINEER. See that big tree there? Well, that was there when I come.

DR. SAM. Well, you don't need to be so cross about it; I wasn't asking no improper questions at all!

MOUNTAINEER. I reckon there's nobody cross here except yourself!

DR. SAM. How did your potatoes turn out here last year?

MOUNTAINEER. They didn't turn out at all; we dug 'em out!

DR. SAM. Can I stay here all night?

MOUNTAINEER. Yes, you kin stay right where you air, out on the road.

DR. SAM. How far is it to the next tavern?

MOUNTAINEER. I reckon it's upwards of some distance.

DR. SAM. How long will it take to get there?

MOUNTAINEER. You'll not git there at all, if ye stay here foolin' with me.

DR. SAM. How far is it to the forks of the road?

MOUNTAINEER. It ain't forked since I been here.

DR. SAM. Where does this road go to?

MOUNTAINEER. It ain't gone anywhere since I been here—jist stayed right here.

DR. SAM. Why don't you put a new roof on your house?

MOUNTAINEER. Because it's rainin' and I can't.

DR. SAM. Why don't you do it when it's not raining?

MOUNTAINEER. It don't leak then.

DR. SAM. Can I get across the branch down here?

MOUNTAINEER. I reckon you kin, the ducks cross whenever they want to.

At any moment, Dr. Sam, whose mother came from Arkansas, would stand on a chair and sing his favorite song (but, of course, this was only after the fifth drink). He learned it from his Uncle Sam.

> I had a cow that slobbered bad
>   Down in Arkansas,
> I spent all the money I ever had
>   Down in Arkansas,
> Carried her to old Doctor Smith's
> Asked him what to do for it
> He said teach that cow to spit
>   Down in Arkansas.
>
> There was a wedding on our street
>   Down in Arkansas,
> A girl named Oats married a man named Wheat
>   Down in Arkansas,
> As they walked down the aisle, you see
> The piano played on the minor key,
> They played "What Shall the Harvest Be?"
>   Down in Arkansas.

I knew a man named David Crockett
    Down in Arkansas,
He carried his false teeth in his pocket
    Down in Arkansas,
He went stirring around and around
He hitched up his horses and drove them to town
The darn teeth bit him when he sat down
    Down in Arkansas.

Had a girl, her name was Lil,
    Down in Arkansas,
Loved her once, and love her still,
    Down in Arkansas,
Pigeon-toes and hair jet black,
Was so crosseyed for a fact,
She cried and tears rolled down her back,
    Down in Arkansas.

"Waiter," cried out an Arkansas traveler, "bring down my
baggage."
"What is it, sir?"
"A bowie knife, a pair of pistols, a deck of cards, and one
shirt!"

THE PUBLIC AND THE PRIVATE MAN:
JOHN BROWN, ABOLITIONIST

Every man who is in the public eye lives, speaks and does things for that public eye. However, he has another side. They are his personal and family duties and the persons and things he loves.

The famous John Brown made two utterances before he died. There was his public speech made in court after he had been sentenced: this was for the world. On the morning of his execution, he handed his will to one of the guards: this was his last personal statement and a very revealing one. It is about the little things and about the people who made up his personal life.

I. THE COURTROOM SPEECH

I have, may it please the Court, a few words to say.

In the first place, I deny everything but what I have all along admitted,—the design on my part to free the slaves. I intended certainly to have made a clean thing of that matter, as I did last winter, when I went into Missouri and there took slaves without the snapping of a gun on either side, moved them through the country, and finally left them in Canada. I designed to have done the same thing again, on a larger scale. That was all I intended. I never did intend murder, or treason, or the destruction of property, or to excite or incite slaves to rebellion, or to make insurrection.

I have another objection: and that is, it is unjust that I should suffer such a penalty. Had I interfered in the manner which I admit, and which I admit has been fairly proved (for I admire the truthfulness and candor of the greater portion of the witnesses who have testified in this case),—had I so interfered in behalf of the rich, the powerful, the intelligent, the so-called great, or in behalf of any of their friends,—either father, mother, brother, sister, wife, or children, or any of that class,—and suffered and sacrificed what I have in this interference, it would have been all right; and every man in this court would have deemed it an act worthy of reward rather than punishment.

This court acknowledges, as I suppose, the validity of the law of God. I see a book kissed here which I suppose to be the Bible, or at least the New Testament. That teaches me that all things whatsoever I would that men should do to me, I should do even so to them. It teaches me, further, to "remember them that are in bonds, as bound with them." I endeavored to act up to that instruction. I say, I am yet too young to understand that God is any respecter of persons. I believe that to have interfered as I have done—as I have always freely admitted I have done—in behalf of His despised poor, was not wrong, but right. Now, if it is deemed necessary that I should forfeit my life for the furtherance of the ends of justice, and mingle my blood further with the blood of my children and with the blood of millions in this slave country whose rights are disregarded by wicked, cruel and unjust enactments,—I submit; so let it be done!

Let me say one word further.

I feel entirely satisfied with the treatment I have received on my trial. Considering all the circumstances, it has been more generous than I expected. But I feel no consciousness of guilt. I have stated from the first what was my intention, and what was not. I never had any design against the life of any person, nor any disposition to commit treason, or excite slaves to rebel, or make any general insurrection. I never encouraged any man to do so, but always discouraged any idea of that kind.

Let me say, also, a word in regard to the statements made by some of those connected with me. I hear it has been stated by some of them that I have induced them to join me. But the contrary is true. I do not say this to injure them, but as regretting their weakness. There is not one of them but joined me of his own accord, and the greater part of them at their own expense. A number of them I never saw, and never had a word of conversation with, till the day they came to me; and that was for the purpose I have stated.

Now I have done.

II. LAST WILL AND TESTAMENT

Charlestown, Jefferson County, Va.,
December 1, 1859.

I give to my son John Brown, Jr., my surveyor's compass and other surveyor's articles, if found; also, my old granite monument, now at North Elba, N. Y., to receive upon its two sides a further inscription, as I will hereafter direct; said stone monument, however, to remain at North Elba so long as any of my children and my wife may remain there as residents.

I give to my son Jason Brown my silver watch, with my name engraved on inner case.

I give to my son Owen Brown my double-spring opera-glass, and my rifle gun (if found), presented to me at Worcester, Mass. It is globe-sighted and new. I give, also, to the same son $50 in cash, to be paid him from the proceeds of my father's estate, in consideration of his terrible suffering in Kansas and his crippled condition from his childhood.

I give to my son Salmon Brown $50 in cash, to be paid him from my father's estate, as an offset to the first two cases above named.

I give to my daughter Ruth Thompson my large old Bible, containing the family record.

I give to each of my sons, and to each of my other daughters, my son-in-law, Henry Thompson, and to each of my daughters-in-law, as good a copy of the Bible as can be purchased at some bookstore in New York or Boston, at a cost of $5 each in cash, to be paid out of the proceeds of my father's estate.

I give to each of my grandchildren that may be living when my father's estate is settled, as good a copy of the Bible as can be purchased (as above) at a cost of $3 each.

All the Bibles to be purchased at one and the same time for cash, on the best terms.

I desire to have $50 each paid out of the final proceeds of my father's estate to the following named persons, to wit: To Allan Hammond, Esq., of Rockville, Tolland County, Conn., or to George Kellogg, Esq., former agent of the New England Company at that place, for the use and benefit of that company. Also, $50 to Silas Havens, formerly of Lewisburg, Summit County, Ohio, if he can be found. Also, $50 to a man of Stark County, Ohio, at Canton, who sued my father in his lifetime, through Judge Humphrey and Mr. Upson of Akron, to be paid by J. R. Brown to the man in person, if he can be found; his name I cannot remember. My father made a compromise with the man by taking our house and lot at Munroville. I desire that any remaining balance that may become my due from my father's estate may be paid in equal amounts to my wife and to each of my children, and to the widows of Watson and Oliver Brown, by my brother.

John Brown.

John Avis, Witness.

93

JOHN BROWN'S BODY LIES

From Edward Dicey's *Six Months in the Federal States,* written in the second year of the war, one learns what hearing the Union soldiers sing meant to one thoughtful and fair observer:

From the windows of my lodgings, I looked out upon the mile-long Pennsylvania Avenue, leading from the broad Potomac River, by the marble palace of the President's, up to the snow-white Capitol, and every hour of the day almost I was disturbed while writing by the sound of some military band, as regiment after regiment passed, marching southwards. The Germans have brought with them into their new fatherland the instinct of instrumental music, and the bands are fine ones, above the average of those of a French or English line regiment. The tunes were mostly those well known to us across the water—"Cheer, Boys, Cheer," the "Red, White and Blue," and "Dixie's Land," being the favorites. For the war had brought out hitherto no war-inspired melody, and the quaint, half-grotesque, half passion-stirring air of "John Brown's Body Lies A-Mould'ring in the Grave," was still under McClellan's interdict. But yet, be the tunes what they may, the drums and fifes and trumpets rouse the same heart-beatings as in the Old World, and teach the same lessons of glory and ambition and martial pride. Can this teaching fail to work? is the question that I asked myself daily, as yet without an answer. Surely no nation in the world has gone through such a baptism of war as the people of the United States underwent in one short year's time . . .

Dicey made a trip to the front and described how, on his way back to Washington, the ceaseless stream of men marching across the bridge on their way to Alexandria made it impossible to cross:

With colors flying and bands playing, regiment after regiment defiled past us. In the gray evening light, the long endless files bore a phantom aspect. The men were singing, shouting, cheering; under cover of the darkness, they chanted "John Brown's Hymn" in defiance of McClellan's orders, and the heavy tramp of a thousand feet beat time to that strange weird melody. As the New England regiments passed our train, they shouted to us to tell the people at home that we had seen them in Dixie's Land, and on the way to Richmond. Ah, me! how many, I wonder, of those who flitted before us in the twilight, came home themselves to tell their own story?

TWO LITTLE-KNOWN POEMS
ON A NEGLECTED SUBJECT

THE IMPORTANCE OF HAVING A NOSE

'Tis very odd that poets should suppose
There is no poetry about a nose,
When plain as is the nose upon your face,
A noseless face would lack poetic grace.
Noses have sympathy: a lover knows
Noses are always touched when lips are kissing:
And who would care to kiss where nose was missing?
Why, what would be the fragrance of a rose,
And where would be our mortal means of telling
Whether a vile or wholesome odour flows
Around us, if we owned no sense of smelling?
I know a nose, a nose no other knows,
'Neath starry eyes, o'er ruby lips it grows;
Beauty is in its form and music in its blows.

Jolly nose! the bright rubies that garnish thy tip
    Are dug from the mines of canary;
And to keep up their lustre I moisten my lip
    With hogsheads of claret and sherry.

Jolly nose! he who sees Thee across a broad glass
    Beholds thee in all thy perfection;
And to the pale snout of a temperate ass
    Entertains the profoundest objection.

For a big-bellied glass is the palette I use,
    And the choicest of wine is my color;
And I find that my nose takes the mellowest hues,
    The fuller I fill it—the fuller!

Jolly nose! there are fools who say drink hurts
      the sight;
    Such dullards know nothing about it;
'Tis better, with wine, to extinguish the light,
    Than live always in darkness, without it.

A UNITED STATES CAVALRY HERO

On every page of conquest before mechanization, horse and man stand together frozen for a moment of shared time. However carelessly one ruffles the leaves of American history, one cannot help but think of Black Tom, ridden by the dashing Captain May when he charged the Mexican artillery; of Cincinnati who served General Grant so faithfully from Vicksburg to his final triumphant victory at Appomattox; of Traveler, the beloved charger of the South's General Lee, and many, many others. Only one horse, however, was retired from active duty for extraordinary bravery under fire. This was Comanche, sole survivor of the Battle of Bull Run.

It is on record that the worst defeat suffered by the United States Cavalry was the Battle of the Little Big Horn. The Sioux Indians in this battle completely annihilated General Custer and his men. When reinforcements came up, there was but one living thing in that bloody trap. This was a horse, an animal who must have lived through a day of indescribable terror and goes down in the history of the United States Cavalry as one of the most honored of his species. He also had the honor of receiving the first flag of truce at Appomattox.

Custer, who sympathized with the Sioux, tried to conciliate them. He conducted a council under a flag of truce, at which he handed out coffee, sugar, bacon, and other gifts. Sitting Bull received these blandishments with many speeches of thanks, but when Custer, carrying out his orders, tried to persuade him to allow the occupation of his country by the white settlers, the proud Sioux chief snorted with contempt.

"For which," said Custer in his report of the incident, "I cannot blame the poor savages."

The Sioux prepared for war. Washington ordered immediate punitive measures. Under the completely false impression that only two thousand braves had rallied around Sitting Bull's tepee, a combined force of twenty-seven hundred men divided into three separate groups set out to pacify at least seventeen thousand Indians.

The entire campaign of the spring of 1876 was typified by misinformation. Apart from the false estimate of enemy forces, the Army seemed completely unaware that the Sioux were armed with the latest in repeating rifles, which they had been buying up for years. It was common knowledge throughout the territories, but the troopers that rode out after the wily redskin carried the usual one-shot carbine with which the Army was at that time equipped.

The bloody climax came on the twenty-fifth of June in 1876 when George Custer, out in advance of the main body of troops, led two hundred men into the valley of the Little Big Horn. According to the usual intelligence reports, Custer believed he was riding in pursuit of a handful of braves. Anxious to cut the fleeing Indians off, he divided his six hundred troopers into three battalions before entering the valley.

At the Little Big Horn Custer's ill-fated company of two hundred men was overwhelmed by four thousand warriors.

Among the men who fell at Custer's side that day was Captain Myles W. Keogh. Keogh was riding a seven-year-old claybank named Comanche. This horse, trembling and shocked, was found alive on the scene. He was led back to Fort Lincoln where he was nursed back to health. Upon recovery, he rejoined the Seventh for active duty and then, as happens with old soldiers, he was dismissed.

An order was immediately issued as follows;

Fort A. Lincoln, D.T., April 10, 1879

General Orders
No. 7

I. The horse known as "Comanche" being the only survivor, or living representative of the bloody tragedy of the
Little Big Horn, June 25, 1876, his kind treatment should
be a matter of pride and solicitude on the part of every
member of the Seventh Cavalry, to the end that his life
may be prolonged to the utmost limit.

Wounded and scarred as he is, his very existence speaks,
in terms more eloquent than words of the desperate struggle against overwhelming numbers, of the hopeless conflict
and of the heroic manner in which all went down on that
fatal day.

II. The commanding officer of Company I will see that
a special and comfortable stall is fitted up for him, and he
will not be ridden by any person whatever, under any circumstance, nor will he be put to any kind of work.

III. Hereafter, upon all occasions of ceremony (of
mounted regimental formation) "Comanche" saddled,
bridled, draped in mourning, and led by a mounted trooper
of Company I, shall be paraded with the regiment.

By command of Brevet Major-General S. D. Sturgis

ERNEST A. GARLINTON
1st Lieut. and Adjutant Seventh Cavalry

At the age of twenty-eight years, Comanche died at Fort Riley,
Kansas, on November 9, 1891. Up to that time, he had been on
the retired list of the United States Army and had drawn a pen-
sion for almost twenty years.

HORSES ARE A PART OF AMERICA

Dr. Sam used to say to me, "You never get tired of a good horse. He don't fizzle out. You like him better and better every day."

From the day the sun first glinted on the armor of conquistadores along the Mexican border until Henry Ford's invention, the mainstream of American life has borne along by horsepower. Horses towed the heavy barges along the Erie Canal. Horses pulled the Conestogas from one end of the country to the other. Horses in relays carried the mail at breakneck speed, for the Pony Express covering hundreds of miles a day through Indian country. The famous Concord coaches like the Deadwood Stage, hauled passengers and freight from Kansas to the mining camps and new cities of the West. The wealth of the country rode in a pair of saddlebags and a Wells Fargo box. The huge cattle drives from the Panhandle to the railheads up North, could not have been possible without horses.

In the great cities of the East, ambulances, trolleys, fire trucks, drays, and cabs rattled over the cobbles behind teams of powerful haulers. Gentlemen's fancy rigs and stylish ladies' carriages threaded daintily through the streets drawn by matched pairs, or fours, in shiny harness. And if you really wanted to impress a girl, you hurried to the local stable where you hired a fancy fringed surrey complete with high steppin' bay! That was a date!

Man's daily rounds were all part of the day's work for the horse. The country doctor was out in his buggy in all kinds of weather. The circuit judge carried his Blackstone in his saddle-bags. The country politician rode from split-log settlement to split-rail farm, plugging for votes while his mount drew in a cool bucket of water.

The peddler, high on the seat of his caravan, carried the benefits of civilization in the form of pots 'n pans and gossipy news of the outside world to women buried deep in fields of corn or cotton, with a peppermint stick for the youngsters and a cut of fresh plug for the hired hand thrown in for free. The circuit-riding preacher in his broad-brimmed hat and black frock coat.

Armies move on their stomachs but it was the horse and his half-brother, the mule, that freighted the food that filled the stomachs American armies moved on.

In every chapter, on every page, they stand together, horse and man, frozen forever in a moment in time that is theirs to share. However carelessly you ruffle through the leaves, you cannot help but stir up their names in passing:

Nelson, who carried Washington from Mount Vernon to Philadelphia through the blazing fields of Princeton and Monmouth, on to Yorktown where the British standards were finally laid at his master's feet;

Old Whitey, who rode across the Mexican border, carrying "Rough and Ready" Zachary Taylor through the campaign to the final day at Buena Vista;

Black Tom, ridden by the dashing Captain May under Taylor's command, who in May, 1846, at Resaca de la Palma, charged the Mexican artillery and leaping bodily over the guns, sent the startled gunners running into the arms of the oncoming Americans;

Cincinnati, who served General Ulysses S. Grant so faithfully from Vicksburg to the final moment of triumph at Appomattox Court House: a spirited bay with dashing hooves that bore the tall, gaunt president in the black stovepipe hat so gently when he visited the battlefield.

Rienzi, who ran under Sheridan on that immortal ride, carrying him "from Winchester—twenty miles away" to Cedar Creek where he turned defeat into victory;

Old Sorrel, who was ridden by the man whose courage and strength were likened by friend and foe to a stone wall—until that fateful evening at Chancellorsville when caught between opposing fires, he carried General Jackson to accidental and tragic death;

Traveler, beloved mount of a beloved commander, General Lee, who wrote of his faithful charger:

> I purchased him in the mountains of Virginia in 1861, and he has been my patient follower ever since, to Georgia, the Carolinas and back to Virginia. He carried me through the Seven Days' Battle around Richmond, the Second Manassas, at Sharpsburg, Fredericksburg, the last day at Chancellorsville, at Gettysburg, and back to the Rappahannock. From the commencement of the campaign in 1864 until its close, the saddle was scarcely off his back as he passed through the fire of the Wilderness, Spotsylvania, Cold Harbor and across the James River. He was in almost daily requisition in the winter '64-'64; and in the campaign of '65, he bore me from Petersburg to the final days at Appomattox Court House.

It was *Traveler* that Lee eulogized in words that might apply to every horse that ever served a human master. After describing Traveler's physical appearance, Lee wrote:

> Such a picture would inspire a poet whose genius could then depict his worth and describe his endurance of toil, hunger, thirst, heat, cold and the dangers and sufferings through which he has passed. He could detail his sagacity, affection and his invariable response to every wish of his rider. He might even imagine his thoughts through the

long night marches and days of battle through which he passed.

General Custer had with him two horses, *Vic,* who died with his master, and *Dandy,* who had been sent to the rear and so missed the battle. Dandy was later sent to Custer's father in Munroe, Michigan, as a living memorial to General Custer.

That well-known buffalo hunter and master showman, Buffalo Bill Cody, rode a variety of horses during his career as Pony Express rider and Army scout. *Tall Bull* was captured in a battle with Kiowa Indians and was named after the Indian chief who rode him until a bullet from Cody's gun brought him to the end of his warpath. Tall Bull was one of the fastest horses on the plains and Cody won a good deal of money matching him against the other western racers.

He also liked to run another one of his mounts, *Powder Face.* One day at Fort Sedgewick, Cody matched Powder Face against a fast pony owned by a man named Luke North. Since North had mounted a Pawnee lad on his horse for the race, Buffalo Bill selected a small boy who lived on the post, as his jockey.

Powder Face was a nervous, restless animal, hard to manage under any circumstances. The excitement of the race aroused him so that he threw his rider at the starting signal. Then, taking matters into his own four feet, he raced down the course and crossed the finish line, leading all the way. The whole affair was unorthodox, but Cody collected.

He was headed straight for a wagon road, a route undoubtedly familiar to the mule but one that Cody had avoided like poison for fear that the wily Kiowas had it under observation.

Dr. Sam, who loved horses, and would often declare, "Sometimes when I feel lonely, catamount, and dull as a bachelor beaver, I just triampouses off to the stable and sets," was not averse to boasting that American horses "kicked the biggest hoof print in the history of horses ever."

97

WOMANKIND DESCRIBED

In 1872, The *Idaho World* published the following satire on young womanhood and what constituted it. The description was written by a more cynical man than I could ever be:

Take ninety pounds of flesh and bone, mainly bone, wash clean and bore holes in the ears. Bend the neck to conform with the Grecian bend, the Boston dip, the Kangaroo droop, the Saratoga slope or the bullfrog beak, as the taste inclines.

Then add three yards of linen, one hundred yards of ruffles and seventy-five yards of edging, eighteen yards of dimity, one pair silk or cotton hose with patent hip attachment, one pair of false calves, six yards of flannel, embroidered, one pair Balmoral boots with heels three inches high, four pounds whale bone in strips, seventeen hundred and sixty yards of steel wire, three-quarters of a mile of tape, ten pounds of raw cotton or two wire hemispheres, one wire basket that would hold a bushel, four copies of the *(Idaho) World,* one hundred and fifty yards of silk or other dress goods, five hundred yards of lace, fourteen hundred yards fringe and other trimmings, twelve gross of buttons, one box pearl face powder, one saucer of carmine and an old hare's foot, one bush of false hair frizzed and fretted *a la maniaque,* one bundle Japanese switches with rats, mice and other varmints, one peck of hairpins, one lace handkerchief, nine inches square with patent holder.

Perfume with attar of roses or "Blessed Baby" or "West End." Stuff the head with fashionable novels, ball tickets, playbills, wedding cards, some scandal, a lot of wasted time and very little sage.

Add a half grain of common sense, three scruples of religion and a modicum of modesty.

Season with vanity, affectation and folly. Garnish with earrings, finger-rings, breast-pins, chains, bracelets, feathers and flowers to suit the taste. Pearls and diamonds may be added and pinchbeck from the dollar store will do.

Whirl all around in a fashionable circle and stew by gaslight for six hours.

This dish is highly ornamental, a *pièce de resistance* for the head of your table upon grand occasion. But being somewhat indigestible and highly expensive, is not recommended for daily consumption in the home.

Dr. Sam would always keep his peace when a gentleman of this bent came into the Davy Crockett Saloon. He would raise his whisky in a half toast to the nude Chloe over the bar, "Let every man skin his own skunks!"

98

SUCCESSFUL WEATHER FORECASTING

In the 1880's, Mrs. Rhoda Smith of Wayne County, Illinois, established the reputation of being the best weather forecaster in the area. At first her neighbors scoffed at her methods but year after year her planting schedule and harvests were timed just right and she soon had the most beautiful and successful farm in Wayne County. Her method of foretelling the weather was simply this:

Each New Year's Eve, Mrs. Smith took twelve onions, all the same size, and lined them up in the kitchen. The onions represented the twelve months of the year ahead. She then sprinkled salt on each onion and allowed them to stand for three days. At the end of this period, the onions that soaked in the salt represented wet, rainy months, the onions that remained dry and refused to allow the salt to seep in would most certainly represent months that would be sunny and arid. The system worked fine.

AN INVITATION TO THE
ZOOLOGICAL GARDENS

When I was thirteen years old and no longer thought it necessary to hide my interest or amazement in those characters called
women, Dr. Sam and my father would at any moment break
into harmony of a nineteenth-century song which they only
described as "The Stuttering Lover." I found it very embarrassing.

I have found out a gig-gig-gift for my fuf-fuf-fair,
   I have found where the rattle-snakes bub-bub-breed;
Will you co-co-come, and I'll show you the bub-bub-bear,
   And the lions and tit-tit-tigers at fuf-fuf-feed.

I know where the co-co-cockatoo's song
   Makes mum-mum-melody through the sweet vale;
Where the mum-monkeys gig-gig-grin all the day long
   Or gracefully swing by the tit-tit-tail.

You shall pip-play, dear, some did-did-delicate joke
   With the bub-bub-bear on the tit-tit-top of his
      pip-pip-pip-pole;
But observe, 'tis forbidden to pip-poke
   At the bub-bub-bear with your pip-pip-pink
      pip-pip-pip-pip-parasol!

You shall see the huge elephant pip-pip-play,
  You shall gig-gig-gaze on the stit-stit-stately raccoon;
And then did-dear, together we'll stray
  To the cage of the bub-bub-blue-faced bab-bab-boon.

You wish (I r-r-remember it well,
  And I lul-lul-loved you the m-m-more for the wish)
To witness the bub-bub-beautiful pip-pip-pel-
  ican swallow the l-l-ive little fuf-fuf-fish!

Dr. Sam would then put his finger to his nose and add,

          "Love it is a funny thing
              It acts just like a lizard.
            It wiggles up and down your spine
              And nibbles at your gizzard."

BEER

In his later years, all my uncle, Dr. Sam, would drink was
beer, and he was full of information in his usual reflective
fashion. "Buck beer or bock bier," he used to say, "the only
actual change of language here is that one's pronunciation
thickens. We call it bock beer here in America," he said, "because it causes the drinker to caper like a bock goat."

One day I showed him a politician's platform reported in the
Baltimore Sun of July 12, 1858, encouraging "a barrel a year
for every male adult in the city." Dr. Sam approved and told
the following story, which I have never run across elsewhere,
about the discovery of lager beer:

Many years ago a shoemaker, near Bamberg, sent his
apprentice to get a bottle of Bamberg beer, which was sold
at that place; but the boy, not knowing this, went to the
city itself. On returning, he met an acquaintance of his,
who told him that when he would come home, his "boss"
would whip him for staying so long. The poor boy, who
was frightened at this, thought it better not to go home at
all, but took his bottle, buried it under a tree, and ran
away. He went among the soldiers, where he distinguished
himself, so that, in short, he became an officer. When one
day his regiment was quartered in this small town, the
officer thought it proper to pay a visit to his old boss, but

not before he had got the bottle of beer, which he had buried some years before under the tree. When he entered, he said: "Well, Sir, here I bring you your bottle of Bamberg beer that you sent me for." The shoemaker, not knowing what this meant, was told by the officer all about it. The bottle was then opened, and the beer was found to be of superior quality. When this fact was known, some of the brewers built deep vaults, where they put their beer, and called it, after it had lain there some time, lager, which means nothing more than lying (not so; it means the beams in the cellar on which the casks are laid.). The officer afterwards married the daughter of the shoemaker, and drank a good deal of lager beer, receiving in that occupation the assistance of his father-in-law.

LIFE IS LIKE A MOUNTAIN RAILROAD

Dr. Sam, as you will realize by now, was much given to phi-losophizing. His favorite hymn was a chorus by Moody and Sankey from a hymn that described life's railway to heaven:

> Life is like a mountain railroad
> Oh, with an engineer that's brave
> You must make the run successful
> From the cradle to the grave.
> Watch the curves, the fills, the tunnels,
> Never falter, never fail.
> Keep your hand upon the throttle
> And your eye upon the rail.

And his favorite bit of philosophizing, one of the rhyming questionnaires, to which he was addicted:

> What is earth to the sexton? . . . A place to dig graves.
> What is earth to the rich man? . . . A place to work slaves.
> What is earth to the graybeard? . . . A place to grow old.
> What is earth to the miser? . . . A place to dig gold.
> What is earth to the schoolboy? . . . A place for my play.
> What is earth to the maiden? . . . A place to be gay.
> What is earth to the seamstress? . . . A place where I weep.
> What is earth to the sluggard? . . . A good place to sleep.

What is earth to the soldier? ... A place for a battle.
What is earth to the herdsman? ... A place to raise cattle.
What is earth to the widow? ... A place of true sorrow.
What is earth to the tradesman? ... I'll tell you tomorrow.
What is earth to the sick man? ... 'Tis nothing to me.
What is earth to the sailor? ... My home is the sea.
What is the earth to the statesman? ... A place to win fame.
What is earth to the author? ... I'll write there my name.
What is earth to the monarch? ... For my realm it is given.
What is earth to the Christian? ... The gateway of heaven.

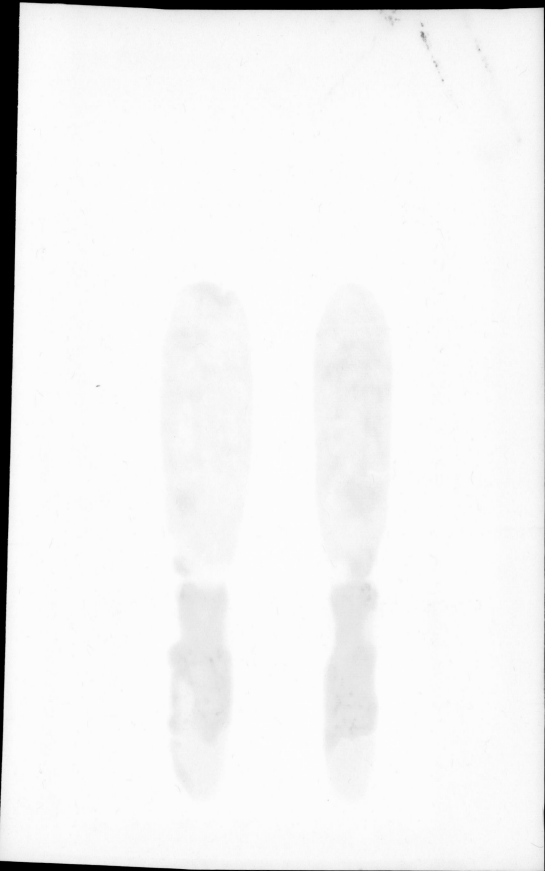

DATE DUE

GAYLORD   PRINTED IN U.S.A.